GOLDYN AKACHI

PRESENTS

THE ART OF LOVE

Goldyn Akachi

The Art of Love

Goldyn Akachi

THE ART OF LOVE

THE ILLUSTRATED EDITION OF THE MOST BEAUTIFUL IMAGES & PORTRAITS BY RANDOM ARTISTS & PHOTOGRAPHERS USED FOR THE LITERATURE, WISDOM, & LIGHT, WRITTEN BY GOLDYN AKACHI & HIS POETRY IN MOTION.

The Art of Love

"Every Rose Has It's Thorns"

Goldyn Akachi

The Art of Love

"Love is the highest level of innerstanding. It is not the type of love that you have been conditioned to believe."

"It's safer to be hated than loved by the world. The world kills what they love everyday, while they live in the midst of hate. Love is a threat."

Goldyn Akachi

The Art of Love

Goldyn Akachi

{The Human Heart is a strange Mystery, full of unstable emotions. Never follow your heart blindly, but rather conceal your heart & guide it with your mind, while opening it up carefully. Choose wisely on whom you decide to hand it to.}

TABLE OF CONTENTS

Introduction

The Real Essence of Love written, illustrated & defined like never before. You thought you knew and mastered the levels, the sacrifices, the joy, the pain, the mis(under, inner, & over)standings, and all the emotions of Love. Well,You thought wrong. Love is Wisdom & Knowledge & if you're not mature enough to handle what comes with it, then Love will destroy you mentally & physically. Take your precious time & really open up your heart and mind to the Poetry in Motion. Read, Analyze, Comprehend, and recieve the fruits given to you as Love shows you it's many characteristics, emotions, actions, & perseverance. After reading this book, Eye guarantee that you will under, inner, & overstand Love a little more & become a better Lover.

Poetry In Motion:
"Seduction"

"Your kisses are like tall glasses of sweet wine,
Every touch from you, brings me to a climax.
So Let us toast to -The Art of Love-,
for you are not on my mind, but rather you are in my mind."

"Fallen Angels"

She may use her body as a Temple or Tool....
She may be after Love, Lust, or Revenge....
Her smile may be Charming or Deceitful....
Her eyes may be Soulful or Soulless....
She may bring Peace or Destruction in disguise....

She may shed Light or she may shed Darkness....
Her sex may be Fulfilling or may be she is
Transmitting her Sexual Demons into a new Host....

Be Aware of Fallen Angels. Do not play in her
Garden and don't even bother to smell her Flowers.

"Dear Pregnant Wombman"

From the heart & soul of every husband & Father out there; Eye was writing this as both a letter to my wife before she gave child birth to our first Sun, as well as an open statement to all pregnant women.

The problem was, my words kept turning back to you and OUR baby specifically. So I'm just going to send this to you my love & God's Will that we will both experience this again if you want to.

You are so beautiful. Eye say it to you nearly every day. But in case you haven't 'heard it' recently, please know this. Please feel it. You are so incredibly beautiful.

The journey of pregnancy, for both a man and a woman, is an amazing one. It's beautiful, it's surreal, and one that is truly hard to understand and fully grasp without having gone through it.

But it's also a hard one.
For her - the body goes through so much during that 9 months. It's growing a human for God's sake! Emotionally, physically - it's an intense experience.

For him and her - your entire world is about to change. Mixed in with all the joy, excitement and anticipation for the future, there is uncertainty, fear, and questions that arise such as, "how the f**k are we going to do this?!!"

The good news is, billions and billions of people before you 'did it'. And it'll ALL be okay! In fact, it'll be the ride of a lifetime.

But Eye digress...

The point of this is you, now, the beautiful, beautiful pregnant woman.

My God, you're the most beautiful being Eye have ever seen.

The way you are.
The way you evolve with our baby over those 9 months.
The way you care for, nourish and love that soul within you.
Eye say with absolute truth my Queen, you have never been so beautiful.

"Vague Voices from up against the Wall"

When she was completely broken & all of her wounds were open...

Goldyn Akachi

The Art of Love

Face soaked in tears, heart shattering for years...

Alone in a dark room, only lit by the pale moon...

Lying on the floor, her tears won't stop anymore...

She hears a vague voice, telling her...wipe away your tears...

Telling her, No matter how hard it is now...

No matter how it seems impossible to survive another night...

Maybe not tomorrow, but one day, you will get over your sorrow...

All of this pain will be a cortex around you that will protect you...

Even if you feel that happiness is not real and you will be sealed...

Goldyn Akachi

The Art of Love

Inside an anguish fate, one day you will be happy
enough to smile heartily...

And these days will just be merely a memory...

You'll laugh loudly, so loud that you'll not hear the
echoes of these days...

Your pain may seem alive, feeding on you to survive...

So cry and cry because one day it will dry...

Bleed your sorrow, so your wounds can heal.

"Colorful Woman"

Maybe If my hair were straighter
or If Eye had blue eyes & a slim petite body
or If my nose & lips were thinner.
If Eye didn't cry over silly things
as well as pick at my hands when Eye get nervous then
maybe, just maybe

you might love me more than her.

Since Eye do not define myself on your standards of beauty
Eye know that Eye am beyond the measure
of the beauty that you've created
out of your own insecurity.

When you Love yourself
You do not have to convince others to love you.

Eye am an original woman
so my originality is flawless!!

"Take Time 2 Ask A Woman About Her Mind"

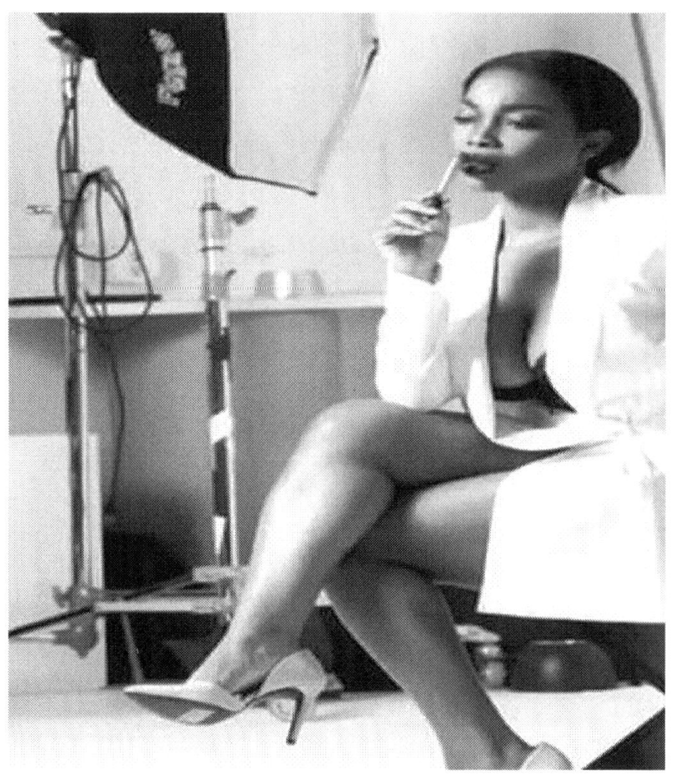

Pause.
And pause. Wait.
Then, ask.
Not in words.
Not in touching.
But ask,

with your constant presence. Powerful.
Feared. Gravely yearned.....

Her dreams and nightmares.

Ask.

In your own style-
Crisp white shirt on a Sunday's glory.
And some cologne for the Gods-
With a hand to your mouth,
And three ears to the land.

Come....

Come. Sit then ask.

Others have only met her at eye level. She gets bored with the ones who want to nest at her bosoms with a shallow mind.

They never do.
She want give it all away.

Not even in this lifetime.
She will never give it all away.
What you know is not what you know, and that is what you came for.
What you seek is hunger, not to be full.
You seek the hunger more than the fulfillment of the woman's mind.

"She Awaits Her Love In Insomnia & Anxiety"

When she is excited for 2morrow she waits for him with every longing, as a child on Christmas Eve, to the point of not being able to sleep.

And when we are afraid of 2morrow too, we can't sleep as a student on test night or like a Mother staying up with her sick baby.
And when there is nothing waiting for her, she stays up all night, and she doesn't sleep because she thinks,

What's next?

She spends the night wondering because she miss, fears, worry, love, dream, & thinks that the night belongs to those whose feelings and thoughts fester like the moon in the dark of the night sky.

So she waits, she waits while visualizes him as the moon and light covered by the night.
................All of a sudden, he rises as the Sun on a bright morning.

He approaches her gently as he wraps his arms around her from behind.

Kisses her softly on the neck while massaging her bosoms. He says,

"Good-morning my Angel" as he smiles, knowing that she watched him sleep through the night as the moon rested in the night skies as well as in her bed.

"What's Next?", he heard her whisper this question in his dreams.

He replies with a grin by telling her softly, "Eye am Real & Eye am not going anywhere unless you want me to & don't love so cautiously where you will make it hard for yourself to accept and experience many different Arts of Love.... You don't have to wait for me....You need to sleep, heal, and recharge yourself. Eye want you at your best, not when you're stress. Worry when Eye am gone, but worry no more because Eye am here."

"Fragile Box"

She didn't know how lost she was,
until she start looking.
And what she found was both beautiful & terrifying.
She's like a ghost, lingering in the dark.
Searching for a world to belong to.

Goldyn Akachi

But some things....
holding her down,
drowning her emotions,
under a frighten cover,
because she knew,
The fragile box,
she kept herself inside,
wouldn't last in this world.
She was too beautiful and too colorful....
To keep her Light dim,
inside of a fragile box in darkness.

She began to love & accept herself in spite of being accepted by the world. She learn to Love herself at times she didn't have the strength to.

"Do you Love me because of what you want me to be and what the world thinks of me? Or do you Love me for who Eye really am, buried inside of this shell?

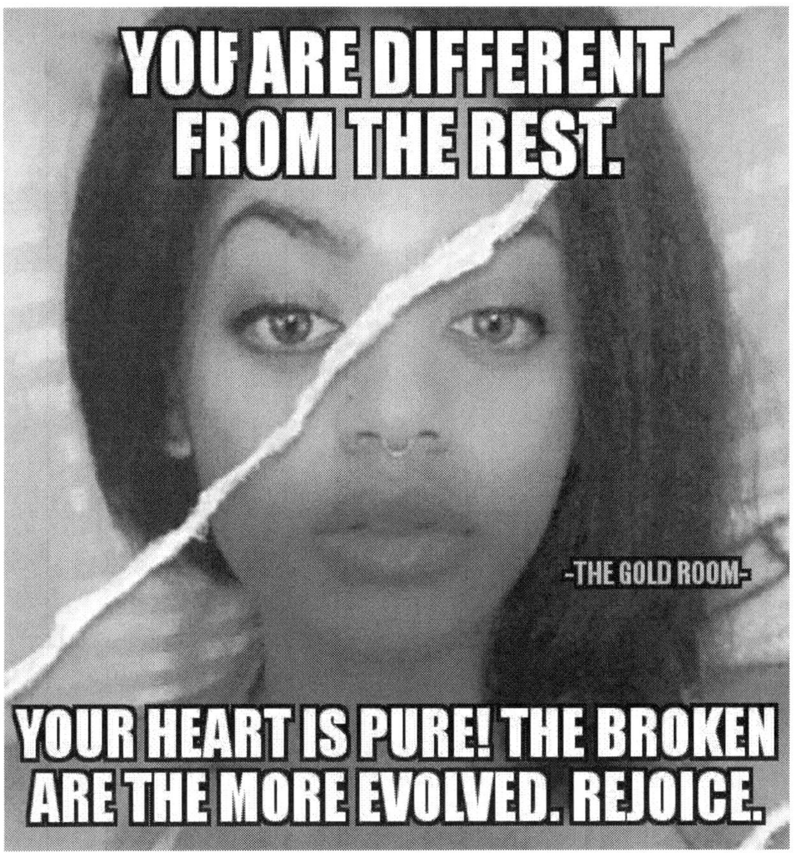

They make fun of us because they don't innerstand.
They never felt what we felt.
But we are more powerful than they are.
Our scars are our accomplishments of survival.
We are glorious!

The Art of Love

We will no longer be afraid.
Only through pain can you achieve greatest.
The impure are the untouched, the spoiled, the unburnt, the unslain.
Those who have not been torn feel no value in themselves and no place in this world.
My Love speaks for the dead that's very much alive.

"Tainted Love"

It happens sometimes......
because we choose to date people we don't know.
(complete Ignorance)

Yet we feel interested in them and motivated to bring us closer to them even before we give them a word.
(crime & punishment)

We tend not to check their background to see if they have healed from past trauma or bad relationships.
(Slippery Slope)

Have they come from a broken home or do they truly know how to love a person or to be loved, when they have never seen or felt the experience.
(That is the question)

We force ourselves to become an attachment to fulfill an empty void or to be someone's replacement while fearing the state of loneliness. We continue to force that person to be everything that we want, but they're not even qualified to fit the description.
(The Illusion)

We settle for death in a relationship because we feel like dying to love them. We hate them to leave us, just not to break the attachment with us for another. So we settle not to die alone, even if we actually hate who's living in our home. We are left numb to the pain.

-An apology without Change, is just Manipulation-

"The Psalm of a Man's Purity & Curiosity"

Eye am a Man....but it always seem like Eye running from myself or trying to find myself.

Eye Love, the way that Eye know how to love, even if it means by not loving myself.

The woman that Eye love, loves me. Well that is what she says. She says my body is sculpted by the Gods and that Eye am her King....but...

Eye am a Man....but it always seem like Eye am running from myself or trying to find myself.

She doesn't like the fact that Eye am attracted to other women, but it is something about the woman that catches my eye. Eye love my woman and the others Eye love differently. Eye can't explain it. Eye wish Eye can have them all but Eye can because someone will always get jealous or hurt in the end. Eye don't even know if Eye am insecure or in need of filling a void in my life. The Love, The Mental Connection, The Touch, & The Comfort of a Woman, stimulates me in a way that every man should feel.

Eye am a Man but.... it always seem like Eye am always running from myself or trying to find myself.

Am Eye a bad man? Eye don't want to hurt anyone. Eye give my woman every part of me & will never put anyone before her. Other women know that and that makes them love me even more. The women that Eye have lost in the past, Eye love them as well, & they wanted me all to themselves & Eye couldn't wrap my heart as a gift, only to be trapped inside of their sealed boxes.

Eye am a Man....but it always seem like Eye am always running from myself or trying to find myself.

What do Eye do? My heart heart is so confused and is filled with wants and desires of different women. Eye melt whenever an attractive woman is in my presence and Eye become everything that she desires in a Man. What's wrong with me....one of these beautiful women deserves me and only me, but honestly Eye can't stop the communication from compatible spirits.

Eye am a Man....but it always seem like Eye am running from myself or trying to find myself.

Eye wonder what it would be like if Eye actually had sex with a woman. Eye love, cherish & respect them so much that Eye am afraid to give them my unbalanced, sexual energy. Afraid to enter their womb & damage what is meant to be pure. Afraid to damage myself even more.

My woman says she loves me. That is what she says all the time. She wants to make love to me but Eye am afraid of what Eye will turn into if her womb is already damaged. Would sex ruin & taint the Love & Respect that Eye have for women?

Eye am a Man....but it always seem like Eye am running from myself or trying to find myself.

"Bloody Rose"

The beauty of life comes with it's thorns.
For those who bear to stick to the rose.
And for those who grow from the labor of war.
And the blood of their love ones painted within the gardens.
To witness the dawn of peace that comes from the roots of conflict.
What's love, if it's not worth holding on to?

The ideal of the Rose (Love) does not secure a relationship.

The Art of Love

Love is built. Your actions and the way you position yourself reflects the type of love you have for that person.

Sometimes we love someone or something just cause....
but when we truly love ourselves, just cause....
It makes us learn to love ourselves unconditionally,
and it causes us to love and balance the right decisions
that we choose to make from within.
A True Rose (Love) never dies.

What causes you to Love?
If that cause, fades away, will the Love fade as well?
Will that Rose die or will it just bleed a little?
That is the question.

Goldyn Akachi

"The Spirit of the Child"
-Warfare of Self-Love living in a Heartless, Adult World-

She was a child who would run freely,
laugh loudly,
and speak spontaneously.

Quickly, she became a Woman.
Quickly, the running around became inappropriate,
and laughing aloud was misbehaving.

The Art of Love

Quickly, she had to think carefully,
about every word she wanted to say.

That innocence in her eyes,
is fading gradually.

Under the microscope of the adult's world,
she tried not to grow up.

Tried to hold on with what was left of herself,
but she wasn't aware.

She's living in a world prevailed by wars,
in a world where humans kill another cause of hate and greed.

In a world where women are just creatures,
A world that has forgotten that the women was created
because Man cant live without her.

In a world controlled by Man
and destroyed by him.

Goldyn Akachi

The Art of Love

In a world prevailed with pain and darkness.
She wished is she died as a child,
her tears almost feel like fire.

She's trying to hold on to a straw,
but inside of her, she's screaming...

"Eye want to drown"
"Eye want to be lost"
"Eye want everything to end"

But outside, she's trying to survive.
She's trying to fight.
But who will win?

The Warrior outside,
or the broken child inside?

"A Mother's Sacrifice"

Eye am raising you alone, the best way Eye know how.
Yet you still act like you are a motherless child.

You disrespect me constantly.

You steal from me even when Eye will give you the
world if Eye can.

Eye take up for you even when Eye know that you are
wrong.

You lie to me and hurt my feelings all the time.

Eye put you before myself because you are my heart
and sometimes Eye love you more than Eye love myself.

Working myself to death everyday just to make sure
that you have the things that you need....& then some.

Eye don't do these things out of love, Eye do it because
it's my duty and responsibility as a mother.

The Art of Love

Eye am sorry that your father is not here with you.
Eye take the blame for that, for not choosing better,
of who Eye lay with.

Eye have not given up on you because Eye truly Love
you & Eye wish that you can see & feel that.

Eye hope that you are not blaming me or anyone for
your situation that you have put yourself in.

It's been a year since you have been in prison and Eye
have sold everything Eye worked for my whole life,
even our house, just to get you out of jail.

They will be releasing you next week.

Eye told you that Eye would never give up on you
because you are my heart and Eye love you more than
Eye love myself.

It's just that,
Eye might not be here when you come home.

Eye am writing you from my hospital bed.

Eye have cancer and Eye can die at any moment now.

Eye wished that you would've kept in touch with me while you were locked up.

But Eye just want you to know that Eye am sorry for whatever Eye couldn't give you growing up.

Maybe by getting you out of jail can make up for that.

Just remember, Eye didn't give you your freedom.

Nobody can give you that.

Only you can free yourself.

Eye am tired now....and it's one thing that Eye want you to know. hhjgiuiuoiio.............................. (flat-line) (she dies while writing)

"Heaven's Letter"

If you are God's personal angel, Eye will live the perfect life just to die to be next to you.

There would be a war at Heaven's gates, because Eye would want you all to myself.

Goldyn Akachi

The Art of Love

God couldn't create or design another woman like you
if he tried....
And God doesn't make mistakes.

My heart has been fulfilled the moment Eye laid eyes
on you.
You floated as you walked and sang a sweet song as
you talked.
Eye know that Eye am in love with you.

Your eyes are like diamonds,
your skin is like Gold.
Love me into yesterday,
so today will never get old.

Tomorrow would never come,
because we are lost in time.
Where the Moon never sleeps,
& the Sun is destined to shine.

Sincerely,

-Love is Law-

"The Woman of the Moon"

The moon is a friend for the lonely to talk to.
So Eye ran just to meet you.

You stay true to your course, but your nature,
you gently influences.

What other body could pull an entire ocean from shore
to shore?

The Art of Love

The Moon is faithful to its Nature,
and your power is never diminished.

They say a woman's true strength is in her silence.
Now Eye see why the Moon is so quiet at night,
but so loud in spirit.

All the great Kings, Pharoahs, Prophets, & Wise
Men have stared and lusted after you every night.

You never left.

From King Tut to Julius Caesar,
From Jesus to Muhammed,
From Mozart to Shakespear,
They all glanced at your beautiful face in the sky.

Did Eye tell you the story of why the Sun loved the
Moon so much, that it died every night just so she can
show her face?

"Sometimes the greatest Action of Love is Letting Go"

"Eye Rise Up Every Morning Because Of Love"

Here Eye am, laying in my bed, restless.
Eye don't want to get up,
My legs have went numb through the night, along with my heart.

It was one of those nights, where Eye have read myself to sleep.
Another love story, where it gives me the hope that Love still exist.
Why do Eye keep punishing myself?

The Art of Love

This will be one of those days....
Where Eye will be a walking dead,
When my body will feel so heavy,
And the tears will blur my vision, but won't fall to my face.

My depression takes over me...
but Love, keeps my heart beating.

Here Eye am, laying in my bed, restless,
with a million thoughts in my head,
with this gut feeling, that this day might be bad.
But despite everything,
Eye choose to get up,
to put my shoes on,
and win the day.
Knowing that, Eye will go through another battle
against this thing called depression.

But today, Eye choose Love...
Those arms, that lifts me up,
That wind, beneath my wings, and that fire, that keeps me alive, burning with passion.

Goldyn Akachi

"The most truthful words are those that are spoken by the eyes.

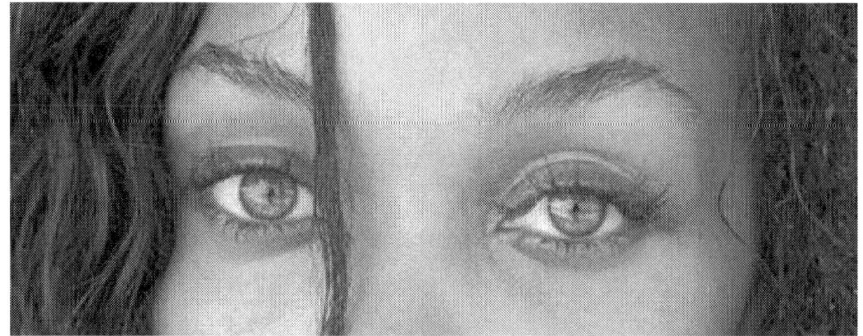

And the most falsely words are spoken by the tongue."

The tongue spoke Love,
but the eyes wondered.
The tongue spoke Love,
but the eyes lusted.
The tongue spoke Love,
but the eyes wanted.
The tongue spoke Love,
but the eyes, fell in love with another.

"How Long Is Love"

If the measurement of Love determines ones faith, then the distance is beyond the eyes can see & what the heart can feel.

"Aa'lonah Monay"

The Art of Love

She wore & carried her beauty as a curse,
nevertheless, her heart was hardened like stones beneath
the dirt.
She gives no facial expressions to the funniest things,
but for the saddest & scariest times, she gives a
heartless grin.
Hell has no fury like a woman scorned,
but for a woman to be unbreakable she must be reborn.
She expresses her emotions in motions of her body,
Like an Angel who dances in hell fire on hard
mahogany.
Compliments of her beauty does not flatter her.
Those are just lustful men, preying and inducing,
For she is in search for a spiritual partner,
Of having two bodies tied tightly together without it
loosening.
She Loved and that Love became lost,
To find it, she has to give her all at any cost.

Goldyn Akachi

A Woman is at her best without worry of being without.
A Woman loves a Man that can take care of her.
It's the Love of Security that she fell in love with, not the Man himself.
Her Love for that Man is built through time & true innerstanding.
Once those two loves entwine,
then you will see her true elegance.

Goldyn Akachi

"Is that the Life you Want, Without Love?"

"Have You Ever?"

Walking in and out of Love
will have you paralyzed from the waist down.
It's like bob wires embracing your legs
every time you walk.

Oh my legs.......

The Art of Love

The pain of agony.
Pieces of flesh slowly ripping off
every time you hurt me and Eye try to leave.
Eye come back to you
because Eye am attached.
Attached to the bob wires
that was lashed out from your heart unto me.

These wires are unbreakable
and so is my love for you.
Just ease up the pain a little
so Eye can walk freely at times
without the strong arm on my legs.

Goldyn Akachi

"Just Hold Me 2Night"

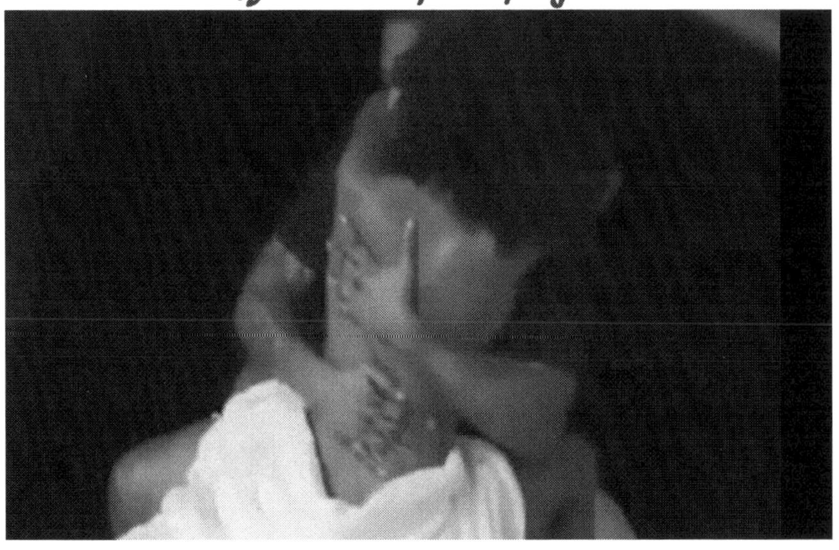

Just hold me tonight
Caress my body over and over.
Let me feel your strong hands all over me.
Allow my skin to melt inside of my bones
as Eye shiver as you touch the soul in me.

From my head to my toes,
You embrace every curve of my body.
Eye fall deeply under your spell,
screaming inside, full pleasure....
ashamed to yell.

The Art of Love

U Love me with no hesitation,
so secure with your touch.
No need for penetration,
that would be asking too much.

Yellow Roses and Pink Daffodils,
Sunflowers and Blue Rain,
In a field, full of Love,
You took away all of the pain.

"Heart of Intense Love"

Step by step,
she fades into nothingness.
Word by word,
she slipped into silence.

The Art of Love

Her life became a deep dark ocean,
And she can't seem to swim.
But she's surviving like a lost item drifting,
towards the emptiness.

Darkened thoughts are hovering around her heart,
bringing her closer into the dark.
She's blindly moving towards it,
because she found no peace in the Light.
She fell In Love within the darkness

Goldyn Akachi

"Lover's Rock"

The wounds were deeper than she thought.
They were engraved in her heart and soul.
The cuts reached her mind
and tore her apart.
Lost in a vicious world

Goldyn Akachi

where Men are smashing the roses,
holding the guns,
and raising war.
Upon us all,
without an end.
Love has become of War,
where women have become Warriors,
who fight for their Love.
Embracing the pain,
while dancing in the rain.
She learned to hold & heal her own heart,
And She also chooses,
which war is worth the fight.

Synonyms of Love:

"Affection".....a feeling of fondness & liking
"Fondness".....the action of finding someone
"Tenderness"..an action gentleness & kindness
"Warmth".......an feeling of affection and comfort
"Intimacy"......an act of closeness, private & sexual
"Attachment". a feeling of sympathy, not letting go
"Endearment"expressing love or affection
"Devotion"....an act of loyalty and enthusiasm
"Adoration"..a feeling of deep love and respect
"Doting"......extremely &uncritical fond of someone
"Idolization"to love & admire,to worship as a God
"Worship"....an action of reverence & adoration
"Passion".....a strong & an uncontrollable emotion
"Ardour"......to love & respect deeply
"Desire".......a strong feeling of want and waiting
"Lust"..........a very strong sexual desire
"Yearning....a feeling of intense longing for
"Infatuation"an intense but short-lived passion
"Adulation".excessive admiration or praise
"Besottedness"a state of being in moral blindness

"Sheer Force of Will"
is stronger than *Love*
as stubborn hope
can't be broken by outside entities.
"The truth of a matter",
"the heart of a matter of fact"
are stronger than *Love*.
Time in it's "infinite wisdom"
is stronger than *Love*...
Love is the strongest "Aphrodisiac."

The 8 Lovers

AGAPE LOVE

Agape:*(ancient Greek) a Greco-Christian term referring to love, "the highest form of love, charity" and "the love of God for man and of man for God".* ***Agape love*** *can be found in the people who dedicate their lives to helping others for the good of humanity. Universal Love.*

Meeting an Agape Lover is kind of rare in this day in age, with so many people that are only in love with themselves.

When you come in contact with the Agape Lover, you will know, first hand who this person is. He/She is very giving and more concerned about your needs rather than their own. You don't have to ask this person for anything or throw mysterious hints at them. They will know everything just by observing you & your lifestyle. Their love is so strong for you that they will put their life at risk just to make sure that you are safe and have everything that you need.

This person rarely gets angry or demands anything from you in return. If this person truly loves you, you would be a fool to turn this person loose. They will go to the end of the world with you and then some. Your true love for this person in return will only make the Agape Lover love you even more. It will become so powerful and unconditional that even in their demise, you will feel their love in your presence.

Agape Lovers are really big on marriage. So if marriage is not your thing or if you don't see yourself being married in the future then the Agape Lover is not for you.

The 16 characteristics of an Agape Lover:

1. They will ***Suffer Long*** for you. Meaning that it takes a lot for them to give up on you no matter how much you hurt them. They're real patient.

2. They are very ***Kind***. Always with a calm and mellow attitude towards people.

3. They are ***Not Envious***. They love to see you succeed and the people around them. They will be the first to support and to congratulate you.

4. They are ***Not Boastful***. They rather praise others rather than themselves.

5. They do ***Not Vaunt*** for themselves. Meaning they will fulfill the needs for others before they fulfill the needs of themselves.

6. They are ***Not Puffed Up***. Meaning they don't flex their superior over others or people who are less than them.

7. Very ***Morally.*** They tend to do what's right that will effect their life and yours in the long run.

8. They are ***Not Easily Provoked***. Some people will try to test the Agape Lover by trying to attack their weaknesses or make them angry, but it will be very hard for them to succeed.

9. They think ***No Evil***. They seem to see pass the evil doings of others and believes that love conquers all pass trauma that cause that person to act in such a negative way.

10. ***Doesn't Rejoice In Iniquity***. Meaning that they do not praise or support anyone who benefits or profits from wrong doings.

11. ***Rejoices In Truth***. They show excitement when things are done right. They believe that a reward is always guaranteed when you play by the rules.

12. ***They Bear All Things***. No matter how much they lose or how much they struggle, they will always take everything with a grain of salt. They will get things done, no matter the sacrifices and losses that they have to live with.

13. They ***Believe what is Good***. If they believe in you, it's no way that you can convince them otherwise.

14. ***Forever Hoping***. Never giving up on the person or people they love. Always wishing for the best.

15. ***Enduring It All***. Loving you until the end. They give Unconditional Love until eternity no matter the situation.

16. ***Never Failing***. A Failed Relationship is not an option for them in anything or anyone they love.

The Agape Lovers

"We will die in the Dark & Love in the Light"

MessiYah was a great Man, full of love and willing to pour it all into the woman he loved.

The woman he loved for three years was named, "AaliYah". She was so beautiful that every time she stepped outside, the sun would dim it's light just so that she could shine brighter. Even at night, the stars would dazzle, as she sparkle in the night.

MessiYah was too, an attractive man, body sculpted by the Gods, and a charming smile that would make any woman melt.

After three wonderful years of love and compassion, MessiYah decided to pop the question. You know, ask for her hand and marriage. He sold what he loved most which was his piano that he used to play, while randomly singing her love songs. He used that money to buy her the ring that she was eyeing a year ago at the mall.

These two love birds sacrificed so much for one another. They were both by each other side when their parents died and also when they both was down and out. It's like, when one didn't have it, the other did, and they made sure they did whatever it took to keep the relationship above water.

Without any doubt or hesitation, AaliYah said, "Yes" when Messiyah asked for her hand and marriage.

MessiYah was so excited and within a month, they both was happily married. They found a nice house in a suburban neighborhood where they felt was suitable to start a family.

MessiYah did just about anything and took every job just to take care of his wife. They were never without.

A year past, and their marriage was stronger than ever.

One night, AaliYah decided to surprise her husband when he returned from work with a candlelight dinner and a rose taped to an envelope. She placed it on a table with chocolate hearts around it.

MessiYah walked in with a crooked smile due to fighting his fatigue from a long day at work. When he saw what his wife had prepared, his face lit up like the fourth of July while blushing in the moment.

He said, "Babydoll, what is this for? What is the special occasion?

AaliYah slowly walked over to him, grabbed his hands, looked deeply into his eyes and told him that he's going to be a daddy.

MessiYah was so thrilled, that he planted a wet, juicy kiss on his wife's lips, picked her up and twirled her around like he had won a million dollars. It was one of the best moments in his life to find out that he was going to be a daddy. In his mind, he started planning things out for his family and couldn't wait to get started.

Quickly, Eight months passed and AaliYah's pregnancy was slowly creeping up into the ninth month.

The pregnancy has been going well since the beginning until AaliYah's last doctor visit. The doctor told her that she might have to deliver early due to some complications with the baby's heart. They both agreed to have the baby delivered early for the sake of the baby's health, but were a little nervous about it.

Within that same week, and days before the delivery, the doctors ran some more test on AaliYah and the baby, and the results came in.

The doctor called the couple in to reveal the results and options that were laid upon them.

As they arrived to the doctor's office, the doctor told them to have a seat, and they both could see the worry and concern in the doctor's eyes. MessiYah even spotted a tear falling from the doctor's eye.

MessiYah told the doctor, "Give it to me straight and do not beat around the bush with me. We will get through it."

The doctor hesitated, with a low shaky voice and told them that it is a possibility that if the baby is delivered, it is a chance that AaliYah or the baby might be severely sick or even die. Also the doctor told them that if she decides to terminate the pregnancy(baby), then AaliYah would be fine.

AaliYah puzzled for a moment, while MessiYah quickly embraced her. They both cried it out while AaliYah cried out and said, "I am not killing my baby!!!, "I am not killing my baby!!!, I will die for my baby!!!"

The doctor felt so bad that she was so sorry to even have put them in a position like that. She told them to go home and discuss this situation privately, and to come back in a couple of days to let her know what they have decided.

Delivery or not, the procedure must be done in a couple of days.

The next day has arrived and they're both are a nervous wreck. AaliYah decided to go ahead with the pregnacy and she was willing to take on the aftermath of what is to come.

MessiYah and her were some people of great faith and they felt that God wouldn't put so much on them that they couldn't bear. They believe that babies are gifts to the world and they would never stand in the way of God's gift.

As AaliYah began the process of having her baby, she was in great, agony pain. With MessiYah by her side supporting and comforting her, the baby was almost ready to come out.

"Give me one more hard push"

"One, Two, Three, PUSH!!!", yelled the doctor.

"It's a girl."

The doctor had to hurry and take the baby right away after AaaliYah held the baby for a minute, and MessiYah cut the umbilical cord. The baby girl needed to be put on a machine right away and have several test ran on her.

Within 30 minutes after delivery, AaliYah went into shock, and just passed out in her bed with the life drained from her face.

MessiYah yelled, "Help, Doctor....Help, something is wrong with my wife! She's started shaking real fast and just fainted! What's wrong with her?"

Come to find out, AaliYah had lost too much blood and suffered from a Hypovolemic Shock that caused a lot of tissue and organ damage.

"Will she be okay?', cried MessiYah.

"She will need a lot of blood", said the doctor.

"Are you a match?"

MessiYah and AaliYah had the same blood type which was very rare.

So then, MessiYah decided to give his wife as much blood as she needed.

The doctor told MessiYah that there is a possibility that she won't make it due to the severe damage to her kidneys and organs, even if he gave her enough blood.

MessiYah was determined and confident that his wife would make it as long as he gave her enough blood. So whatever the doctor told him that was negative, it went in and out of his ears.

As the blood drained from MessiYah's arm into AaliYah, MessiYah started to turn a pale color. He was giving too much blood. The doctor told him that she didn't want him to give all of his blood at once, because this can be detrimental to his health.

"Stop!!!, don't touch me", cried MessiYah.

"I won't stop giving her my blood until she awakens."

"Sir, Sir. She's gone", said the doctor.

"Her heart failed her and it's nothing we can do, I am sorry"

MessiYah heart drop, and fell to the floor with the iv still in his vains. Due to the lack of blood he had, he was so weak that he didn't have the energy to cry.

It's like his world was stripped from him and he was left to die alone.

MessiYah slowly gathered up some strength to raise up to AaliYah's bedside and wispered these words in her ear. "We will die in the Light and Love in the dark."

After that, MessiYah dropped lifeless to the floor, right beside his wife's bed, while blood was still flowing into AaliYah's veins.

Doctors rushed to his side trying to revive him but failed numerous times.

Theories say that MessiYah died from loss of blood and a broken heart which no one could even fathom or explain.

After several months in the hospital, their baby girl was beautiful and healthy.

Her mom, AaliYah, wrote on a piece of paper that she gave to one of the doctors before the delivery; and it said:

"To our beautiful daughter Ariel Ashanti....We love you very much and you are a gift to the world. We are always with you and everytime you look in the mirror, you will see us. See you soon."

Eros Love

Eros: *(Ancient Greek "Love or Desire)* ***Eros*** *refers to "passionate love" or romance. The term erotic is derived from eros. In Greek myth, it is a form of madness brought about by one of cupid arrows. The arrows breaches us as we fall in love by force and hyptosis.*

The Eros Lover is a very attractive and seductive person. They will use their eyes, body, and flirtatious ways to seduce you. Most of the time they are doing these things just to satisfy their own needs.

They can be a little jealous and they love to be in competition with other attractive people. It becomes a game of love with them and they will do everything in their power to become the victor in the end.

The Eros Lover cannot be classified as good or bad because of their sum of life-preserving instincts that are manifested as impulses to gratify basic needs. Also as impulses to protect and preserve the body and mind.

If the Eros Lover really loves you, your relationship will be very romantic and passionate compared to others. So don't just think that these lovers are evil and out to destroy you sexually, spiritually, and mentally. You just have to beat them at their own game and make them surrender to you.

The phrase "Love is Blind" refers to the Eros Lover. That is their weakness. When they're in Love, they see no evil.

The 10 Characteristics of the Eros Lover

1. ***Human Love*** is directed toward the other person for its own sake. (Selfish Love)

2. They seek ***Personal Contact***.

3. They want to ***Gain,*** to ***Capture*** by every means.

4. They desire to be ***Irresistible***.

5. They desire to ***Rule***.

6. They have ***Little Regard For Truth***.

7. They seek to be ***Served***.

8. They ***Cannot Love Their Enemies***.

9. They ***Cannot Tolerate Rejection***. When rejected, they turn to hatred, contempt, and calmuny.

10. They Create themselves to an end. They nurture an ***Unrealistic Ideal*** and ends in ***Narcissism***.

The Eros Lover

"Brooklyn's Bridge"

"Have you been across the bridge to Brooklyn's?"

"No, I haven't been to New York, but I want to go."

"I am not talking about New York, fool, I am talking about that fine gal named Brooklyn, who stay over that bridge by your cousin's house."

Darrius laughed, "My bad bro. Nah, I haven't even seen or heard about her. If she's fine, you already know that she will be mine eventually."

"Yea right. Do you know how many brothers that have tried to get at her and failed?"

"It don't matter, all women love money and the finer things in life. So once I wine and dine her and get what I want, then you can have my left overs."

"If you say so bro," while Jacob laughs at his friend Darrious', confident remarks.

Across this 'half of a mile' bridge, on the outskirts of Houston, Tx is where a young and beautiful woman named Brooklyn resides. She just made 21yrs old this pass February. The 25th to be exact, and couldn't wait to be on her own.

She left her mother's house after she finished her college courses that she was taking to become a proffessional Hair Stylist, so she can open up her beauty shop that she invested in.

Brooklyn is a very intelligent woman and has a good head on her shoulders, but it seems that she struggles with loving others and accepting it from others as well. Her dad walked out on her mom when she was 13yrs old due to struggling and depression. I guess he couldn't take the pressures of the world anymore. Her dad was from Brazil, so I guess he fled back there, who knows....but that situation still effects Brooklyn till this day with so many unanswered questions.

This upcoming Saturday, there will be a party held across Brooklyn's bridge. It will be hosted by Brooklyn and a few of her friends that decided to come together to parlay.

Brooklyn asked her friend Alexis, (who is a stripper) to go shopping with her & had in mind, to go shop for the most seductive and revealing outfit at the mall.

Brooklyn's body was very fit and curvy. She knew how to catch the eyes of men by the way she allowed her clothes to expose every aspect of her body. Men would even pay just to take pictures with her. She would lead some men on into thinking that she liked them, but was only attracted by the way they came out of their pockets for her. She dined at every fancy restaurant there is and recieved every extravagant gift, that a man can give. Some of the things she received from these men, she gave it to her mother and friends.

She owed so many men dates and second dates, and never responded back to them after she got what she wanted from them. She felt that if she can control a man so easily, then she didn't really need that man, because she considered him weak. She always have known that most of these men are weak behind seductive women and they only think with their d*cks.

Even though Brooklyn flirted with a lot of men, she was very careful on who she had sex with. She didn't have that many sex partners. She believe in keeping a Man wanting and fantasizing about her. That way she can keep finessing them. Don't get me wrong, she did have sex with whomever she wanted to just to satisfy her needs.....no strings attached, and that's how she liked it.

The day came and the big party was tonight. It was going to be held at a clubhouse in Brooklyn's neighborhood. The decoration was really extravagant and the bar was set with all kinds of fruity drinks.

Darrious and Jacob were ready to attend the party even though they were uninvited guess. Darrious was very eager to see how Brooklyn looked and if she lived up to the hype.

10 'o clock was the time and the party over at Brooklyn's Bridge has just begun. The ladies are all dressed up looking spontaneously sexy, while the guys are all dressed to impress and looking to flirt and pounce like wolves to the sheep. Brooklyn and her friend Alexis were the center of attention like always. Everywhere they walked, the eyes of the crowd would follow.

Darrious and Jacob finally pulled up at the party around 11:30pm. Waiting outside the door and smoking their cigars like successful business men. It was a tatic they used to draw the party to them while they pimped the parking lot.

Note that Darrious and Jacob are two very handsome brothers with a lot of swag. They definitely stand out from the rest of the guys at the party.

While Darrious and his friend stood by his gold, 2020 BMW X6, it caught the attention of Brooklyn and Alexis. The two women came outside the party and asked the guys are they coming in.

"Why are y'all still sitting out hear", said Brooklyn, as she gave a flirtacious look.

Darrious said, "We're just chilling for now babydoll, and we really don't like crowds. What's y'all name?"

"Hmm, Wouldn't you like to know. Why don't you come in and dance with us if you really want to know our names.", Alexis jumped in and replied.

The guys quickly put out their cigars and followed the girls inside of the party.

Alexis grabbed Darrious by the hand while he was checking Brooklyn out. Took him to the dance floor and started grinding all on him.

Jacob was one of the good guys and very shy around women. Brooklyn noticed that from him and a man's weakness is her biggest strength to confirm that she's in control. She flirted with Jacob but she knew that Darrious was giving her the eye of want and desire. So she played civilized like the good woman.

The whole time that Brooklyn was talking to Jacob, Darrious were breaking his neck trying to keep a tag on Brooklyn's whereabouts.

Alexis really liked Darrious and she basically stayed around him the whole night, while following him outside to his car from time to time.

Jacob was such of a good of a friend to Darrious that he told Brittany that Darrious wanted to meet her. He literally told her that Darrious was a grest guy and she should get to know him. Brooklyn stated that she thinks her friend likes him more and that she would just let Darrious choose on who he really want. Jacob already had a girlfriend and told her that she was the only reason why they decided to come to the party. Brooklyn was flattered.

As the party and the night came to a end, Darrious and Alexis met Brooklyn and Jacob at his car.

Brooklyn said, "I was so glad that you guys took time out of your busy schedule to come to our party. We really enjoyed y'all."

Darrious quickly responded, "Most definitely, thanks for invited us without an invite."

He reached out and grabbed Brooklyn's hand, and planted a gentle kiss. Alexis looked bothered and jealous. "You're going to call me right?, and you're going to be my new man."

Darrious laugh, "Yea, Eye will call you", while giving Brooklyn the side eye of seduction.

Jacob just sat back with a grin on his face, knowing that this is about to be some conflict between the two friends.

Brooklyn has always been a competitive person and if she knows that a guy that she finds attractive is someone that her friend likes, she will try her best to take that man away from her. That's just the type of woman she is.

The guys finally got in the car and drove away from the party. Darrious was very impressed on what he had saw from Brooklyn. Jacob told him everything that him and Brooklyn talked about and also he even got Brooklyn's number for him.

"Damn, Brooklyn is fine as hell. Her friend Alexis was cock-blocking the whole time and she wouldn't leave me alone. That chick crazy and a freak", said Darrious.

"Why didn't you just tell her that you wasn't interested in her?"

"You don't tell a female that. Why do that and you can have them both?", Darriouis laughed. "I am still going to call her....and Definitely I will call Brooklyn."

A couple of weeks past and Darrious finally called Brooklyn. That was his law; to never call a female as soon as he gets her number. He believed it showed desperation.

"Hello Brooklyn?", "It's Darrious."

"Darrious Who?", said Brooklyn as she answered the phone irritated.

"From the party, I lost my phone and finally bought a new one", Darrious said.

"Oh hey, aren't you suppose to be calling and hooking up with my friend, Alexis?"

Darrious said, "Nah, I want you and I thought you caught the vibe and the way that I was looking at you."

"Yea, I caught that, I just didn't think you were man enough to go after what you truly want," Brooklyn said aggressively.

Brooklyn was the type of woman where she was the aggressor in all relationships and she loved to dominate and control a man. Darrious was the type to let a woman think that she's in control, but on the other hand, he is really controlling her through his clever ways.

The two talk on the phone for atleast a week as they were getting to know one another better. Brooklyn has never met a man that wasn't pushing the issue to see her. It was very strange to her. She even asked Darrious was he gay or something, because most of the men that she have met, have always tried to have sex with her.

Darrious just played it cool and took his time with Brooklyn because she seem like a prize worth waiting for.

This kind of situation was all new to Brooklyn, especially for a man being concerned about her childhood on how she grew up. She always avoided getting too personal with a guy, but the way Darrious' charming character was, she had no choice but to spill the beans.

As time when on, the two became close and they kinda grew on one another. Brooklyn became attached to him, but still had her doubts in men generally.

One day she decided to get one of her girlfriends, who also worked at the stripclub, to come and seduce Darrious. It was a setup to see if Darrious would entertain the situation and become weak unto the flesh.

This situation back fired for Brooklyn because Darrious ended up having sex with her friend while knowing that Brooklyn had her sent to him. His response to Brooklyn was that he thought she was a gift from her, and why would she send a woman like that to him if she were serious about them being together.

Brooklyn was furious, but she really had that coming since her and Darrious were not officially dating. She told Darrious that he was no different from any other man out there, but curiously asked him why he never tried to have sex with her.

He told her that he doesn't respect or love them other women who give it up so easily, and that sex is just sex. It has no meaning to him and that he wants to be with a woman that he can genuinely make love to.

In Brooklyn's mind, she came to the conclusion that Darrious was more sexually attracted to her friend than her. So since Brooklyn is a competitive woman and do not believe in having a woman take someone she likes, she ended up pushing the issue of Darrious being her Man.

That same night, she invited Darrious over for a very passionate night and the two made love.

After that, Brooklyn became very possessive and controlling. She even flaunted Darrious around her friends like a badge of honor, while literally saying that, at the end of the day he chose her.

Darrious notice the change of behavior in Brooklyn and was very concerned. He even told her to chill out from time to time and that she doesn't have to put a leash on him.

Brooklyn really didn't trust Darrious, especially from the last incident and was really plotting to get back at him. It's like she wanted to be with Darrious and then again she didn't want anyone else to have him. Especially anyone she knew, and she knew mostly every female across the bridge.

Darrious decided to take a break from Brooklyn by just advoiding her phone calls. He started putting in voluntarily overtime hours at his job, so Brooklyn wouldn't think he was with another woman.

Brooklyn got so furious that Darrious was advoiding her that she went up to his job to see if he was really there.

It was around lunch time as Brooklyn drove by his job.

At Darrious job, they have a picnic, lunch area outside where the employees eat.

So as Brooklyn drove by, she saw Darrious sitting with one of his co-workers which was a beautiful woman such as herself.

Oh, the jealousy and envy rolled up Brooklyn's spine and she drove off with all kind of wicked thoughts scrambling in her mind.

You see, Darrious is a flirtacious and a very charming kind of guy who really is a good man. The friend of Brooklyn that he slept with, was really an old girlfriend from years ago where from time to time they will still hook up. Brooklyn never knew that. And the woman she saw him laughing with, was just a co-worker, nothing more.

Brooklyn had a plan to get back at Darrious, and to get his attention.

She dicided to call Jacob, Darrious' friend. She made it like it was an emergency and that she needed to see Jacob right away.

Jacob being the nice and caring guy, he agreed to meet up with Brooklyn at her house.

When Jacob got there, Brooklyn was teary-eyed like she had been crying for hours.

Jacob asked, "What's wrong?"

Brooklyn told him that Darrious was cheating on her and that he hit her.

Jacob comforted Brooklyn and told her that he was sorry to hear that and to not stress, and that he got her.

Brooklyn took that as a gateway to make her move.

She turned her head as Jacob held her tightly, and starting kissing Jacob on the lips.

Jacob untangled himself slowly from Brooklyn and told her that he has a girlfriend, and that this wasn't right.

Brooklyn continued to force the issue and continued to hug and kiss him. She told Jacob that she always wanted him instead of Darrious, but the timing was all wrong.

Slowly Brooklyn was undressing herself and at the same time Jacob was pulling her clothes back up. It was a tussling situation.

Out of nowhere, Darrious pulled up at Brooklyn's house as he saw Jacob's car parked outside in front of it.

Darrious got out of the car and hurried to the door. Knocked and the door slid open.

It looked as if Jacob had giving in to the temptaion of Brooklyn's beauty, because he was on top of her while both of them were half naked.

Darrious yelled, "What the f*ck are y'all doing?"

Brooklyn screamed, "Get up off of me and I told you to stop."

Darrious was no fool and knew that Jacob didn't force the situation and that Brooklyn was very deceitful. So Darrious just walked up out her house and went back to his car.

Brooklyn hurried and ran after him.

"I'm sorry, I'm sorry, I was lonely and I needed someone to talk to. I felt that you didn't want me anymore and I called Jacob to comfort me.'

Darrious wasn't trying to hear that.

Then Brooklyn change her toned and said to him, "how does it feel now, to be cheated on?"

"You're crazy", said Darrious.

Jacob looked confused and just got in his car and drove off. He hated confortations and drama. He always was the guy to let people think what they wanted to think.

An hour pass and Brooklyn was still trying to convince Darrious that it was all a misunderstanding.

Darrious told her that they're over and that he doesn't have time for this love/hate game that she is playing.

Brooklyn stated that Men don't leave her, she leaves them. She threatens Darrious that if he breaks up with her, then she will make his life miserable.

Darrious got into his car, let the window down and yelled, "The world does not evolve around you and you cannot force anyone to love you. My life will never be as miserable as yours and you better stay your *ss away from me."

Afterwards, he drove off, across Brooklyn's Bridge to never turn back there again.

PHILIA LOVE

Philia: (Ancient Greek, often translated "brotherly love". In Aristotle's Nicomachean Ethics, philia is usually translated as "friendship" or affection. The complete opposite is called phobia. The friendship is a strong bond between the two who share common values, interest or activities.

The Phila Lover or love is based off of a true, successful long-term relationship. It is very important that you are friends and feel the same way with the other person as well in order to build this kind of love.

You will need to enjoy doing things in common and sharing similiar interests. This does not mean that you have to share everything in common but think of your friendship as one of a kind, meaning that the relationship is very capatible from the rest.

The Philia Lover is the best type of person to build a relationship with. They will bring trust and companionship.

This is very important in friendships, because this is what allows your relationship to be healthy and long lasting. Both people are able to benefit from and contribute to the relationship. This is how deep friendships are formed that help you better yourself and grow as a person. Such a relationship is also important because it allows you to have someone that you connect well with and enjoying spending time with.

The 8 Characteristics of the Philia Lover:

1. Very ***Useful.*** This is when there is a connection and you're getting something from that. It's leading to something that you desire such as a job, business contact, on even growth of Elevation.

2. ***Pleasurable.*** You can receive a lot of self pleasure from this person that involves just hanging out somewhere you like or just being in their presence.

3. ***Virtue.*** A deep connection and includes you considering the welfare of the other person.

4. ***Balance & Equality.*** They are very balance and fair on everything they do. This is so that no one is getting more out of the friendship/relationship than the other. No one is being tooken advantage of.

5. ***Trustworthy.*** Always dependable and will do whatever they can for you.

6. ***Empathetic & Compassionate.*** Even when you are going through something that they have never experienced, they will be there and do their best to comfort and innerstand you.

7. ***Honest.*** No matter what, they will tell you the truth on how they feel.

8. ***Room for Independence.*** This is the kind person that will not smother you or feel some type of way when they are not the only one getting all of your attention. They will give you the independence and freedom to go hang out with other people.

The Philia Lover

"Can We?"

I am sitting here thinking about what happened last night. Seriously I don't even know what actually happened. It was like a rush of an emotion that took hold of me.

I feel so embarrassed and I felt like it was my fault. I should have controlled myself in that heat of a moment.

We have been best friends for like 5 years and we have never looked at one another in such a way. I can't even face you or look into your eyes at the moment so this is why I am writing you this letter:

Dear Christopher:

I love you so much with all of my heart and you know that. When I am not around you, I feel empty like my other half of myself is missing. It's like you have become my drug that requires me to inject at least one dosage a day to function completely.

What I am trying to say is that, is it possible for us to start dating or do you think that it will destroy our close bonded friendship?

I am willing to take that risk because I know that it will kill me inside to see you become intimate with someone else. Every time you use to tell me about your past relationships with other women, it made me cringe inside, hoping you will break up with them. But as long as I knew that you were happy, I accepted the reality that you was in love with another woman.

Now that you are single and available at the moment, I don't want to miss out on another opportunity that could be a part of my destiny. You probably never knew that I felt this way about you and it probably made you hesitant on even taking it there with me. Maybe you was afraid as well....who knows.

Even if you decide not for us to date, i will still love you the same and will not treat you differently. Just know that I truly love you and do not want to lose you over any foolishness or any uncomfortable feelings that we may have towards one another in the future. Please get back to me asap and whatever decision that you decide to make, I will understand and accept it.

Love You Always.

PHILAUTIA LOVE

Philautia: *(Greek, romanized: philautia) means "self-love"*
The root of ***philautia*** *denoting self-love and arising from it,*
a general ***type of love****, used for* ***love*** *between family, between friends,*
a desire or enjoyment of an activity, as well as between lovers.

Philautia Love is a type of love that is within onself. "Philautia is essential for any relationship, we can only love others if we truly love ourselves and we can only care for others if we truly care for ourselves. Love always start within oneself before anything.

It is very hard sometimes to point out the Philautia Lover because so many people are putting on this face to cover up the lack of love for themselves. These type of people are not Philautia lovers. You can tell by how they carry themselves after they have put everyone before them. They will play the victim of why they are in the situation they are in because they are too busy putting everyone needs before theirs. A Philautia lover will never do that because in order for that love to be pure and sincere, they will always make sure that they are taking care of first, and not expecting anything in return from the ones they have shown love to.

Self-love can be good and bad depending on your own feelings. If you don't have much love for yourself, you are most likely going through a depression. Loving yourself is always a process and you have to be patient with it. Whenever you go through things or even when people try to tear you down, you will sometimes have to start over by learning to love yourself again. That's the wisdom and power of the Philautia Lover.

8 Characteristics of the Philautia Lover:

1. An essential element of ***"self-esteem"***. They embrace the postive aspects of self-love that allows them to pull themselves up when they are down.

2. ***"Love."*** Is what they take very seriously. If they say that they love you, they mean it and will show it unconditionally, even if that same love is not given back to them.

3. Shows ***"Regard"*** for self and other people feelings.

4. ***"Self-Acceptance."*** Whatever reality they are in at the moment, they accept it and embrace it including how they look, act, or have.

5. ***"Very Understanding."*** They know how to reach a common ground with anyone or any situation.

6. ***"Passionate."*** Whatever they decide to do or who they decide to love and care for, they take it very seriously and will give their all.

7. ***"Conceited"*** at times. This can be looked at in a good way because it is very hard to tear down a

philautia lover when they think so much of themselves. It's their motor that keeps them going.

8. ***"Narcissistic"*** love for oneself, a destructive self-centered approach to life with all it's negative attributes.

The Philautia Lover

"Seeking Philautia (Self-Love)"

Dear younger self:

Life hasn't always been easy for you, but not because life is hard (though it sometimes is). It's because you are hard on yourself, and you are your own biggest critic. You strive for perfection and have yet to realize life is full of beautiful imperfections. You're 15 and want to be just like everyone else. As I peer into the past, I have so many things I want to tell you.

I want to tell you to put that hair straightener down and let your thick curls run wild. So what if the other girls in school all have straight hair? Your curls make you unique.

I want to tell you that what you wear doesn't matter and to quit begging your parents for name-brand clothes. When you graduate from college, you'll work at a gym where you get to show up in sweats every day—so spend your money on something more valuable, like traveling. Oh, how much you'll get to travel in your life! Every road trip you go on and plane you board will open your eyes to a different culture and view of the world. Your travels will help you figure out who you are and what you want to be.

Keep at it because as long as you are moving forward, you are growing and becoming more you.

I want to tell you to quit comparing yourself to those around you. Not everything you see online is what it seems. Only the "like" worthy aspects of people's lives tend to get posted online so never feel low because your life doesn't compare to someone else's highlight reel. I want you to ignore what others are doing and instead focus on living the best life you can. Comparing your life to someone else's will only set you up for disappointment because chasing after what someone else considers important will never satisfy *you*.

I want to tell you to stop worrying about what the number on the scale reads. Scale weight is just a number—it does not define who you are as a person. I also want you to stop worrying about what you look like. Women's (and men's) images are distorted and photoshopped in magazines and all over the Internet. It's so easy to hide cellulite, thin out body parts and remove blemishes to achieve a flawless look. And it's not just models and celebrities who get brushed up anymore, soon you will have access to tons of apps that alter what you actually look like before your picture is posted online. There's a filter for everything these days (quite literally on the Instagram app) but I hope you are able to see past the filters and view life with a clear lens of what is real.

You have insecurities, you're clumsy, you've made mistakes, you've had plenty of moments of self-doubt, and you've been sad more times than you'll ever admit. But all of that will make you stronger and has made you who you are today.

I want you to know that everything gets better and you will find your way. It took some time but you finally learned that you were young and impressionable when the world said you should look a certain way and be something you're not. I sought approval from everyone else but not myself, for so long. I'm writing to tell you that those years have taught me some important lessons that you —my younger self—will eventually share with others like you.

You've learned that you're not the only person with insecurities. Whether people choose to embrace their insecurities or not, the annoying thoughts are still there. You'll eventually learn to embrace all your flaws and this is when you'll truly begin to grow and break through your own limits. One day you'll admit to yourself how frightening it used to be to express yourself aloud to others. When you spoke about your emotions, your voice would crack and your thoughts jumble up, so you chose to bottle your feelings. Writing and reading will be your outlet. You had body image insecurities, because at such a young age you were bombarded with photos of stick-thin women. Yes, your legs and butt have always been bigger than most. I promise one day you'll turn those two glorious aspects of yourself into assets. One of the best things you have done for yourself is start a blog and share your thoughts to inspire and encourage as many people as possible to be confident in their own bodies.

STORGE LOVE

Storge: *familial love refers to natural or instinctual affection, such as the love of a parent towards offspring, family members, or people who relate in familiar ways that have otherwise found themselves bonded by choice. and vice versa. The natural love and effection of a parent for their child.*

Storge love is never forced. It comes so natural that it becomes that person's personality and way of life. Storge is one such concept that aims to explain the love parents feel towards a child, and vice versa. While not limited to the parent-child dynamic, storgic love is defined loosely as a familial love. While it can describe attachments between the siblings, it is most frequently used to describe the love between the parents and offspring. Taking a broader view of this idea, storge is a love of unity. It is the type of love that binds the families together, races, clans and the social groupings.

Characteristics of the Storge Love:

Storge Love is not based on a desire, It is not fleeting. It is not impermanent. It is, for lack of a better expression, love at its most basic and pure.

Storge Love is "**A Bond That Grows":** The love between a parent and child is instantaneous and indescribable. Talk to any first time parents and ask what they are feeling and you will likely hear them say, "it was love at first sight." Intense as this might seem, part of the excitement of being a new parent is knowing that the bond and love will intensify further over time. While this experience is natural, this strength and depth of this love can feel equally unnatural and unexplainable.

Simply put, the love you feel for your child is core component of your make-up as parent, it is part of your wiring that grows from the moment you conceive to when you depart this world. In more simple terms, you're primed to form instantaneous bonds with your child and there is no logical explanation as to why and how. Fortunately for many anxious first time parents, your child is equally likely to build this bond from within the womb and their first appearance in the delivery room. This phenomenon is storge at work.

The Storge Lover

"The Love Behind The Love"

Diamond has been single for every Valentine's Day most of her life but one, and that was four years ago before giving birth. So on this Valentine's Day - she rejoiced! Yup, you read right, she Rejoiced! (Even though she didn't celebrate or believe in the holiday like her male friend & everyone else did.)

Instead of all her your time, attention, and energy being focused on that one person tomorrow, she chose to focus on her family and friends - those that would have her back whether she was single or not. In a way, she had more Valentines than someone with a sweetheart! Every year near or on Valentine's Day, she would schedule dates with her daughter, parents, siblings & her two besties, and they would have an awesome time eating junk food and watching movies together.

She always believed that Valentine's Day shouldn't be just a day of romance, & love! And there were different kinds of love besides eros (being IN love with someone). There's storge (family love).

She knew it sucks to look around at other couples. In fact, she knew a lot of people that tried to find someone this time of year just so they won't be alone on Valentine's Day. She was glad to be still single because she didn't have to stooped that low. After all, would you really want to be in a relationship with someone who depended 100% on you for their happiness and self-worth? Of course not! It was completely unhealthy to her. She believe that people shouldn't fixate on the idea of a relationship when their not in a healthy place & it was no point into rushing these things. She allowed herself to be built up by those who gave her storge love which influenced her to become one with herself after her breakup. She sensed no growth in her past relationship.

Valentine's Day came around and Diamond spent the day inside of her own home with her daughter. They sat and ate junk food while playing all kinds of board games as well as video games.

Chelsea was 4 years old but a very well spoken child. She had a mind of her own and was very observant to what goes on around her. She asked her mom why wasn't she out on a date with her boyfriend, and was she taking her to her grandmother's house.

Diamond responded by hugging her daughter tightly while telling her that they are are going to spend Valentine's Day together, because there is no one she loves more than her. Chelsea was so excited and she told her mom that there was no person that she loved more than her as well.

As the day went on and the night time approached, Diamond decided to have some intimate converasations with her daughter. She expressed on how much she loved her and how her daughter changed her life for the better. She apologized to her for not giving her a stable, loving, and caring father. She admitted that she had made some bad decisions in her life but she never regretted having her as a daughter.

Diamond was very sensative and open when it came to her daughter. Many times before when she felt broken and helpless, she would just lay in bed with her daughter crying laying her head on her chest. Chelsea would always tell her, "It's okay mommy, don't be sad, it will get better. You're the best mommy in the world and I am proud of you." That always made Diamond feel better and loved so much even when she felt as if no one actaully loved her.

Before the day ended, Diamond made it clear to her daughter that no matter what happens from this day forward that she will always put her before anything in the world. She mentioned that their love for one an other would never be broken and no matter how young or old, she will always have her back and be there for her no matter what.

Diamond kissed Chelsea on the forehead and they danced into the night until the stars feel asleep.

PRAGMA LOVE

Pragma**: Pragma is a kind of practical* ***love *founded on reason or duty and one's longer term interests. Sexual attraction takes a back seat in favor of personal qualities and compatibilities, shared goals, and "making it work"*

Pragma is also known as Pragmatic love or **Enduring Love**. This is the kind of love that values practical aspects of a relationship as the most important and driving force. This can mean that the pragmatic lover weighs up what they consider to be important traits for their relationship and their partner, and bases their view of whether love is desirable or not on whether there are sufficient reasons for it to be useful and valuable to them.

Being this kind of lover can be helpful in many ways, because the qualities the pragmatic lover has chosen for their **ideal partner** are based on genuine belief in what can sustain a long-lasting relationship for them. When they meet the right person, they do not need to waste any time wondering whether it can work, because they already have a very definite idea that it can, so doubts are less present in a pragmatic lover's mind.

However, there are downsides to this kind of love, for the pragmatic lover thinks of themselves and also for their partner. These downsides for the partner come in the form of expectation that they will live up to a certain pre-defined role in their pragmatic lover's mind. This can be disconcerting and may be even become painful if the partner of a pragmatic lover feels misunderstood, stifled or as though they are a disappointment to their partner as the two get to know each other better.

By its very nature, love and relationships offer deeper and deeper insight into each other's personalities over time, and it may be that a first impression or first few months of a relationship reveal a very different person to the person underneath, as the two people become more comfortable with each other and see more and more aspects of each other's personalities, moods and lifestyles.

The pragmatic lover, in turn, may feel intense disappointment or even something like betrayal if they find that their partner is not exactly as they had expected or imagined them to be in any important way. This can lead to problems early on in the relationship in which nobody is at fault.

Pragmatic lovers love to feel useful to their partner, and vice versa, and it is this feeling of everything moving towards a practical and useful end that fills them with satisfaction. This they see as being the way a functional relationship should be. The upside of thinking this way is that, when their relationships do work, they are indeed lifelong and wonderfully fulfilling ones, which the daily mundanities of life together do not deteriorate but rather strengthen.

Characteristics of the Pragma Lover:

A ruthlessly pramatic person can fall in love, however that term is quite risky for those who like things planned. The best description is that they can develope love for someone and then love them after all requirements have been met (at least to some degree).

A person who is pragmatic is concerned more with what should be. A pramatic person's realm is results and consequences. If that's where your focus is, you may want to apply the word to yourself.

Pragma Lovers are also:

1. **Down to Earth**
2. **Earthy**
3. **Hardheaded**
4. **Logical**
5. **Practical**
6. **Realistic**
7. **Very Opinionated**
8. **Visionary**

The Pragma Lover

"Even Death, Can't Do Us Part"

Henry & Martha are both 75yrs old and have been married for 54yrs. They both live alone in a small town in Texas called Lily Rock, where they own lots of farm land. They have 6 Children, 21 Grandchildren, & 15 Great Grandchildren and their family is very close and well connected.

This is the life that they both dreamed for and desired when they first dated years ago. It wasn't all peaches and cream in the beginning, but they both knew what they wanted and was willing to make sacrifices.

As teenagers, while dating, Martha parents did not approve of Henry because he was what they called back then "A Stray Cat"....meaning that he was a fatherless/motherless child who wondered the streets, scratching to survive. He never knew his parents and was giving up for adoption. He spent most of his childhood living in multiple foster homes, because he kept running away. He was a child who coundn't stay still in one place for long, so when he was around 15, he made the streets his home.

Martha had a different lifestyle. Hers was more civilized and glamorous as they may say. Her family wasn't wealthy or rich but compared to what Henry had experienced & have seen, it seemed as if Martha's parents were rich.

Every other Saturday, Martha would go to the Carnival with her parents where they would have all kinds of festivities that they enjoyed from circus clowns, live entertainment, magic, petting zoo animals, and refreshments. This is the place where she met Henry.

Somehow Henry made his way to the Carnival every weekend where he would survive off the left over food and drinks that people left behind. He didn't have any money so he found ways to sneak in. Everyone thought he was just away from his parents at times. He always had his eyes on Martha everytime he seen her, but never approached her. He remembered seeing this gorgeous girl with the same yellow beret in her hair, walking with her parents all the time; and maybe that was the real reason why he never had the courage to approach her. He didn't want to be seen as a peasant.

This went on on for about two years that Henry would see Martha at the Carnival with her parents, until one day he caught Martha alone by the lemonade booth.

"Excuse me Miss!, Excuse me!, Henry yelled out.

"My name is Henry, what is your name?"

Martha never had a boy approach her in that manner as if they found her interesting, so she just ignored him. Henry insisted on getting her name, so he reached down in his pocket and paid for Martha's lemonade. That seemed to catch Martha's attention and she told him that she was grateful, and her name was Martha. She then realized that Henry was a nice guy and was not a crazy, strange person who was just being annoying.

Henry then started a conversation, telling Martha all about himself on how he grew up, while she just sat there listening to him out of curiosity. Martha always loved and admired a person who is very talkative and outgoing because her parents were really protective and didn't let her go out much.

These two spent about hours walking & talking while getting to know one another until they bumped into Martha's parents. Martha introduced Henry, but her parents looked at him like they were disgusted like why on earth are you associating with this trash. Before Henry could even speak, Martha's parents grabbed her forcefully as they walked off, heading to the car to drive home.

Henry was left in shame and in dissapointment because it had been a long time that he actually had someone that he could just open up to.....especially a beautiful girl.

When Martha and her family arrived home, her parents gave her a full lecture on trying to date uncivilized boys and told her that she should not be focused on dating anyone. Her focused need to be on leaving for school this fall. Martha's parents were planning on sending her to a all girl's college in New York. They wanted her to leave Texas and to start a career there.

Martha didn't like this idea at all and wanted to remain in Texas. She was 17 and considered herself as an adult to make her own decisions on where she can go and who she can talk to. She really connected with Henry and often spoke highly of him during the debate with her parents.

After that they told her that they wasn't taking her to the carnival anymore and didn't want her associating with the likes of Henry.

So time when on and Martha's parents never took her to

the Carnival for the rest of the summer, but every Saturday, Martha would sneak out of the house and meet Henry there.

One special day at the Carnival, Henry sat with Martha and told him that he wanted her to be his girl and eventually his wife. He told her that he wanted a big family, (something that he never had) and would do anything as a Man to take care of her. He told her that he would face anyone and any obstacle that would come in between them being together. Even though Henry didn't have anything to offer her, there was no limit of what he could accomplish with her being by his side.

Martha would then find herself falling in love with Henry from every moment they spent together.

Martha sacrificed her whole college career and went against her parents will, just to be with someone she loved. Her parents ended up kicking her out of the house at the end of the summer because she refused to go to New York.

From the motivation of Martha being his girl, Henry found a hard labor job that would then pay for his own little house where Martha would eventually move in and they would become married.

Every night after work, the two would just lay next to one another in bed and dream with their eyes open on what they wanted in life with one another. It's like they were soulmates and wanted the same success in life. When Henry didnt' have it, Martha would find work to make up for what they didn't have. It's like they were teammates going after that championship.

Today, they are both 75yrs old, and when Henry bought his first little house in Lily Rock, Texas, he was 17yrs old. That was 58 yrs ago to this day, and they still have that little house on their land but have built another big house around it for their family.

One night, they both decided to go into the little house and lay down next to one one another. (This was the same house and bed that they both laid in 58 yrs ago.) Before they went to sleep, they brought up the same ole memories on how they met at the Carnival. Martha wondered what ever happened to her parents and told Henry that if she could go back in time that she wouldn't have changed anything.

They both found it amazing and an act of God that all the things they had dreamed for as teenagers, came true. It seemed as if their lives have been complete, and their kids were all planning to raise their families together on the 60 acres of land that they own.

As the night went on and the stars shined through the darkness of the night, Henry and Martha fell asleep as they held one another, not knowing that this would be their last night together on earth. They both died in their sleep with a smile on their face.

LUDUS LOVE

Ludus: *game or school in Latin. Those who see* ***love*** *as a desiring to want to have fun with each other, to tease, indulge, and play harmless pranks on each other. The acquisition of love and attention itself may be part of a game.*

Ludus, or Playful love was described by the Greeks as the kind of love felt by young lovers or children. Ludus is defined as "sport or play" so this type of lover tends to view love as a game. They will take pride in having multiple conquests and will find it extremely hard to commit to one person, after all they're all about the game and excitement that comes along with a new partner. This type of love has the potential to turn into Mania, which is characterized by addictive behaviors and dependency, or to Pragma, in which you choose a lover based on whether he or she is good for you or not.

People who enjoy love as Ludus get the most out of having fun with the partner (or partners) they are with, it's not uncommon of them to play harmless pranks and to want to be together a lot, having many indoor or outdoor activities that include laughter, socializing and most of all, require attention.

Characteristics of the Ludus Lover:

Ludus lovers are fond of playful flirting and they need attention. A common way to practice Ludus is going to bar and flirting and dancing with strangers. As this will rarely lead to a meaningful relationship, especially if you are not looking for one.

People who engage in Ludus find themselves always trying to outwit their partner and can be ***narcissistic liars***, since they love nothing more than playing around with the other person's feelings. They rarely get attached, but they pay extra attention to see if their partner is getting emotionally attached for 2 reasons, one it makes them feel good and feel a sense of accomplishment. And number 2, if they notice that their partner is getting emotionally attached, they can use this to their advantage, and thus ensure that they will not be the ones getting hurt. All this ***lying and deception***, for people who experience love as Ludus, is just meant to always have the upper hand, even though they are normally ***cheaters*** and always like to date more than one person at once, they will feel very offended if they find out one of their interests is doing the same.

While it may seem like Ludus lovers are ***inconsiderate***, it's because narcissism is like that. It makes a person feel superior when they get away with whatever they are trying. But if they are the ones outsmarted, it will hurt them more deeply than the ones they are usually playing. This makes Ludus seekers very prone to mixing their love with mania.

Once they have mixed these two up, it will drive them crazy. If someone who experiences love as Ludus finds out one of their partners is seeking someone else, they will work extra hard for this person. This is the reason Ludus lovers are so careful when stepping into relationships, if they are the ones making the wrong moves it might make them start an **obsessive behavior** that could go as far as stalking, just to make sure that person does not abandon their side, and hurt their ego even more.

It does not however mean that the Ludus type are ***jealous***, if they feel someone else is after their partner, it will even make them enjoy the fact that they are winning.

Ludus people are, in the bottom of their heart, seeking the thrill of a new relationship. For this reason they have a ***wide range of physical tastes*** in partners, they are not very picky when it comes to picking out a new target for their game. Everyone experiences butterflies and excitement when they start seeing a different person, but Ludus type lovers need it to be able to enjoy a relationship, hence when it starts to evolve and they find themselves starting to get bored of the person they seek amusement elsewhere. This is what makes it especially hard for people to enjoy Ludus to be able to start a committed, long-term relationship.

Since Ludus lovers will go out with many people during their ***sexual peak***, it is very likely that they will acquire a lot of knowledge about themselves and what they want. So, every time they are going out with someone new, they will be able to notice what they like and what they don't. Meeting all these people will also build them a huge network of acquaintances and friends. This means that once they move on from the Ludus type of love and are finally ready for a relationship it is very likely that it will be long lasting one (Pragma, or practical love), and it will probably be with someone with whom they started going out for fun.

Recognizable traits of someone who is embracing Ludus is that they are normally very guarded. Since they need to always be in control, only on rare occasions will they share deep, personal thoughts or so much as a lot of information about themselves. They are always on the prowl for new things and are not ready to commit or develop deep feelings for anyone.

If you notice you are going out with someone who is a Ludus type, you should know you are not irreplaceable and might as well just have fun too. Enjoy their company and live in the moment, because if you are expecting them to change for you, you are mistaken. Ludus lovers are ***not fond of expectations*** as just go with the flow, as soon as they start feeling they might be pressured into a relationship they are not seeking, they will leave and find someone else in a matter of days. Ludus types rarely find themselves crying over a relationship that is no more. ***"Nothing serious"*** is their motto.

The Ludus Lover

"My Experience With Ludus" (Warning)

When I first read it in passing, I thought Ludus was a playful kind of love like I imagine Martin and Gina from the t.v. show Martin, or Chris Pratt and Ana Faris have. However, when I researched a bit more it's actually more of a game-playing and manipulative kind of love that doesn't really sound like love. It means "the game" in Latin. You know, "dont hate the player, hate the game," mindest.

It's about lack of commitment and is usually attributed to young lovers or children. Ludus is the flirtatious love that finds people at bars. Ludus is the guy still on Tinder even when he's in a relationship. Ludus is the guy you flirt with at work and accidentally make out with at the Christmas party. Dancing with strangers, almost a playful substitute for sex. Ludus wants as much fun as possible and sees marriage as a trap.

To me it seems that Ludus isn't love, actually. It is a shadow of love, masquerading in its attraction, playfulness and excitement. Maybe there is a place for Ludus in your youth, when you don't know what you want or are trying to navigate feelings and desires. Or maybe it's the early stages of a relationship where you flirt and still hold your cards close to your chest. But Ludus can't be forever. You can't forever be the girl that manipulates guys to get something, or the f*ck boy that is stringing along multiple women. I think it's closely related to Eros, but rather than the attraction to the person like in Eros, it's attraction to the thrill in Ludus.

I'm not here to tell you how to live your life, but if you're the manipulator with someone that wants something real, go find someone else who wants the same thing that you do. If you're in one of these type of relationships, or being manipulated and you don't want to be, it's time to talk, leave or re-evaluate. You deserve someone who wants to have a proper go like you do.

Good luck, lovers. Never again will I date a Ludus.

MANIA LOVE

***Mania:** love that is obsession, it becomes mania. Stalking behaviors, co-dependency, extreme jealousy, and violence are all symptons of mania*

Mania. This refers to an obsessive love style. These individuals tend to be emotionally dependent and to need fairly constant reassurance in a relationship. Someone with this love style is likely to experience peaks of joy and lots of sorrow, depending on the extent to which their partner can accommodate their needs.

When one is in the throws of new-love (falling madly in love), one is experiencing the extremes of *passion*. In such a state, *commitment* is either assumed or viewed as something to be discussed later. **In a manic state, the current moment reigns supreme**. Intimacy, or sharing personal insights, is viewed as unnecessary. The two individuals click so naturally, they feel as if they have everything in common. If differences do surface, couples are content to agree to disagree; or minimize the significance of the contrast.

Characteristics Of The Mania Lover:

Mania, often found within the context of Bi-polar disorder, is an euphoric, sped-up mental state. People in a manic state require less sleep. They tend to make grand plans in conjunction with their critical thinking. They feel powerful and larger than life, often being irritable or aggressive towards others. Manic individuals are ***impulsive:*** particularly in spending money and having sex.

Recognizing that new-love resembles mania is beneficial to know in and of itself. To supplement, however, I will put forth three manifestations of ***manic thinking*** within the context of new-love:

•*Confidence in the stability and longevity of the relationship*

•*Belief that nothing could outweigh the good in the relationship*

•*A 'deal with it later' approach*

Confidence

While in this love-manic state, 'rose-colored glasses' outlooks dominate. The discounting of any doubtful reservations occurs. "We will last," is the thought, supported by a euphoric feeling. This is opposed to a "Will it last?" thought accompanied by a negative emotion, which is a thought process one would see in non-manic lovers.

It is important to comprehend the over-confidence people in this state have in the futurity of the relationship. There is not a single doubt. ***They couldn't imagine things going bad even if they were told to do so.*** For the couple, their eventually not being together, or not being in love, is completely nonsensical.

Belief

If anything negative presents itself (a bill, a car wreck, a diagnosis, feelings for an ex etc.) it is discounted. ***The two in love view anything that may pose a threat to their relationship as minuscule compared to the strength of their love.***

Couples may take turns squashing naysayers the other volunteers (being in the early stages of intimacy, the two discuss their biggest fear: threats to their relationship). To the man saying "I still think about my ex," the woman may say "That's normal, it will pass, we are okay." Thus, in mere moments, the concern is satisfied: the man feels understood, validated, and put at ease. The woman is charmed the man opened up to her and warmed by their intimacy. They continue to view their relationship as bullet-proof.

It is possible, though, that neither deems it necessary to bring up potential problems in the first place. They view their love and bond as invincible.

Deal with it later

Someone in a manic episode may purchase something exorbitant on credit, then tell themselves that they'll deal with any fallout later. In a manic state, the individuals confidence in his/her own ability to take care of issues (including financial situations) is heightened.

As is the case of someone in a manic episode, ***those in new-love are not concerned with future consequences.*** Couples may purchase a house, get corresponding tattoos or become each other's cosigners; in addition to other things that typically involve long-term planning.

In this love-mania, passion and pleasure between the two in the relationship is intensely felt *and* sought after. ***Passion and pleasure are sought after as if going slower would drain the feelings; everything must be done immediately.***

Passion's Climax:

It is prudent to reemphasize that those in a love-induced manic state are at the heights of passion; and that passion's ultimate manifestation is sex. The feeling of love induced mania is intense and stimulating (love has, in fact, been referred to as a drug).

For this reason, a key indicator of manic love is unprotected sexual intercourse. It is possible that neither pregnancy nor birth control has been discussed; yet as the two continue to grow in passion they may engage in unprotected sex (to feel as close to the other person as possible [closeness is felt less when protection is used]). Any reservations regarding birth control or potential pregnancy are cast aside. The act of intercourse feels urgent; having a discussion may damper the passionate feelings. Any misgivings are discarded with a "We can handle anything, we'll deal with it later, I love her/him so much it doesn't matter" attitude.

The hourglass of manic love:

The *urgency* felt between two in the throws of manic-love is telling. ***The truth is, there is a clock on the feeling of being in maniacal love. Manic-love fades in time, as does passionate love.*** In a way, those in a rush to do things together (and not be away from one another) are aware that the powerful feeling they are experiencing will not last.

The Mania Lover

"Matrimonial Acrimony"

Dennis & Jada have spent the last 12yrs married and they have 2 beautiful children. Dennis is a very successful entrepreneur that involves him being a relationship expert and counselor, with his wife being his full supporter and business partner.

Dennis always betrayed himself to the public as the perfect

ideal man that every woman should have. His teaching tactics and strategies is based on bashing and blaming the man in the relationships while victimizing the woman. Basically saying that it is always the man's fault on why she acts out in the relationship.

Many women idolized and loved Dennis, and to him, he had them right where he wanted them to be. It started off by him flirting a bit and having harmless interactions with other women, but it came to a point where women would just throw themselves at him. He was the intimate, listening ear to these women when they had relationship problems and they knew that Dennis would make them feel better about their situation. Dennis had the charm and charisma to match and comfort their vulnerabilty. This is when he would prey on his victims, eventually have sex with them.

Jada knew that the career that her husband had would

draw all kinds of women in, but she trusted him to the fullest and would never in her life think that Dennis would ever have an affair with another woman. She ignored the personal, late night phone calls from other women, and the nights that Dennis would leave the house, claiming it was about business.

Every time Jada's intuition would kick in, that would have her very suspicious, Dennis would make her feel as if she was being jealous and out of her mind. He would make her feel like the guilty one and would sometimes grab her aggressively to put fear in her.

From the outside looking in, you would think that they had the perfect marrige. At least for those who actually knew that they were married. Most of the women that Dennis had an affair with didn't even know that he was married or had any children. Dennis also felt that he had his infidelity under control and could have these spontaneous relationships waiting for him anytime he needed them.

Time when on and Jada realized that Dennis was doing to much and her consciousness was getting the best of her of what Dennis was doing. Dennis had a huge platform on social media and Jada saw a lot of women claiming to have relationships with him. The one that hit her the hardest was when she saw a woman's photo of herself laying in the bed that Dennis and her shared. This made Jada furious and she brought it up to his attention.

Dennis was very intelligent in a way that he could manipulate any situation. He convinced her that the woman photoshopped the picture and that she has been stalking him for a while, hoping that she would make his wife mad when she saw her photo online.

Once again, Jada fell for Dennis' game....or did she?

Jada had skeletons of her own by secretely being with other men on the side without Dennis even knowing. She felt in her heart that Dennis was cheating on her but needed physical evidence to justify what she was doing, so she wouldn't feel wrong if she was to be caught. She just played the role of the jealous and concerned wife and had the mindset of if he wants to play that game, then so be it. Note that she always felt that as long as he didn't put another woman before her, then it was no point into leaving the mansion and finer things that they had together.

Even at his spoken word seminars, she would just play the role as if they were the perfect couple and watched him expose other men for cheating, and not being man enough to even know how to love their women properly. As long as the money came in, she tolerated everything.

All that changed until one of Dennis' mistresses came to the forefront with live videos of them together, having many affairs. She even had proof of her being pregnant by Dennis and being forced to get an abortion. It was no way for Dennis to deny this allegation because the woman went to the public. This scandal flooded all social media platforms and urban radio stations. It even caught many celebrities attention. The same male celebrities that Dennis spent time bashing about cheating on their spouses. This whole incident went viral and they destroyed Dennis' image as being a narcissistic hypocrite.

Jada then found out about this. Her and Dennis had their arguments and Jada left the mansion for a couple of days while realizing that she rather gain than lose everything. She wasn't going to allow another woman to take her place. She felt that she had worked too hard for their brand, to give up all that she had for some jezebel. Dennis knew that Jada had secrets of infidelity and told her that he really didn't care as long as they had an mutual understanding that they both will remain faithful for now on.

They both then decided to come up with an apology strategy to the media and their supporters because they didn't want to taint their image or have their brand destroyed completely. So they went religious with it and use God to justify the sins that were made in their relationship. It was now about forgiveness and how to make a marriage wither through all the storms they endured. They even wrote a book about their marriage with both of them on the cover.

Deep down inside Dennis was furious that another man had touched his wife sexually, so he literally beat his wife behind closed doors.

Jada took it all in and basically follow along with the plan, just so she can keep living her lavish lifestyle.

Many years later after all the chaos, abuse, lies, fame, fortune and infidelities in their marriage. Jada decided to leave Dennis and take half of everything. She even left an explanation to the media and their supporters stating:

***"I left my marriage, not because Dennis kept cheating,
not because he abused me mentally and emotionally.
He actually FINALLY was doing everything right.
I left because I'm no longer in love. He's not
the guy I want anymore. It's sad that I actually
waited for him to do everything right, but it's too late.
I guess I'm ungrateful. He should've loved me
when I loved him. I wanted to leave this Matrimony Acrimony,
meaning that our marriage was making me become bitter,
angry, ill feeling, bad blooded, while having animosity, hostility,
enmity, spleen, malice, spite, peevishness, and venom.***

"Pain will leave once it's finished teaching you. Afterwards, you will learn to embrace it."

"**Eye Trust You** is more powerful than **Eye Love You**, because you may not always **Trust** the person you **Love**, but you can always **Love** the person that you **Trust**."

"The Sparkle always Depends on the Flaws of the Diamond"

-TWIN FLAME-

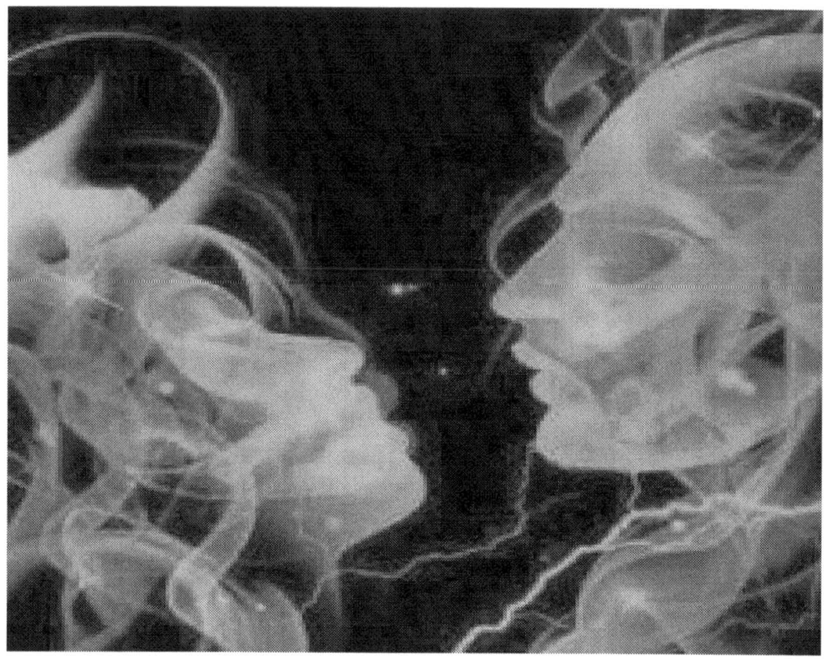

A lot of people may not know what Twin Flames are and many might use this term just because it's trending or sounds good. More often, we want and force our companions to be much more than they are meant to be. We create our own reality with the person we choose to be with, just because it feels right at the moment. We have to be really careful when we put these labels on people that we hardly know.

A Twin Flame is a person who you feel connected to not just on a physical and emotional level, but also on a soulful or spiritual level.

Our Twin Flames represent our friends, lovers, and teachers in this life. They are the people we dreamed about and yearned for our whole life. They the suns to our moons, and the light to our darkness.

Twin Flames are also our mirrors in that they reflect back to us all of our hidden fears and shadows, but also our true inner beauty and strength. In this way, our Twin Flames open the door to tremendous emotional, psychological, and spiritual growth.

You can also have more than one twin flame but these different twin flames consist of different aspects in your life concernig people and certain relationships

21 Signs Of Knowing That You Have Met Your Twin Flame:

1. ***You feel a strange, inexplicable sense of "recognition" when you meet the person.*** This might manifest itself as déjà vu, or an unshakable feeling that you've known this person before, or are somehow "meant to be together."

2. ***You have a feeling that they are going to play a very important role in your own development,***without knowing when, why or how.

3. ***You've established an immediate, intense connection*** with them that is invigorating and shocking at the same time.

4. ***You feel as though you've finally found a "home"*** or safe place with the other person.

5. ***You are able to be your <u>authentic self</u>***– flaws and all – without the fear of **<u>rejection</u>**, persecution or judgment with them.

6. ***You both embody the yin and yang,*** in other words, your dark side is balanced by their light side, and their dark side is balanced by your light side.

7. ***You feel a sense of expansion with them,*** as though you are larger than your limited identity.

8. ***They make you a better person***, and you make them a better person.

9. ***When together you are both bonded but free, attached but unattached.*** In other words, you still

maintain your freedom even though you might be in a relationship with them.

10. ***You are finely tuned to their energy***, and they are finely tuned to yours. This means that you are both very conscious of the present play of energy (whether happy or sad, angry or forgiving, open or withholding) present in the connection. You're both therefore highly empathic with each other.

11. ***You feel as though you have been waiting for this person your entire life.***

12. ***You both connect deeply and mirror each* other's *values and aspirations for life*** beyond surface similarities.

13. ***Your twin flame is a mirror of what you fear and simultaneously desire the most for your own* inner *healing.*** For example, if you are a highly-strong person, your twin flame will most likely be relaxed and messy. If you like to play the victim, your twin flame will be a strong character who refuses to give you pity or sympathy to perpetuate your complex. If you are creatively repressed, your twin flame will be a flourishing artist. In this way, our twin flames challenge and infuriate us but also teach us important lessons about our fears, core wounds, and repressions.

14. ***Your childhoods were polar opposite.*** You were raised in very different ways, which led to the development of opposite childhood wounds that you now have the opportunity to mend.

15. ***One of you is more soulfully mature than the other*** and often serves as the teacher, counselor or confidant within the relationship.

16. ***You are taught important life lessons*** such as forgiveness, gratitude, empathy, and open-mindedness by them and with them.

17. ***The most growth you've ever experienced has been with them.*** No other friendship or relationship has transformed you as deeply as this one has.

18. ***Your connection is multi-faceted.*** In other words, your twin flame is likely your best friend, lover, teacher, nurturer, and muse all at once.

19. ***Your twin flame doesn't try to change you.*** They accept you for who you are and what stage you're at and encourage you to do the same for yourself (and vice versa).

20. ***You can be truthful with each other about anything.***

21. ***Together, you both feel driven towards a higher purpose,*** whether spiritually, socially or ecologically.

After reading this, you might still have a few questions about Twin Flames. So after doing a little studying and observations, I will shed some Light on the more common questions that most people may ask.

Are twin flames meant to be lovers?

No, not necessarily. There is no such thing as a cookie-cutter twin flame relationship. Some twin flames are lovers, while some twin flames are best friends. You don't have to feel sexually attracted to your twin flame for the connection to be legitimate. It's perfectly normal to have a platonic relationship. People let their sexual lust deceive them often into thinking they have a twin flame.

Does everyone have a twin flame?

Yes, it's quite likely that everyone has a twin flame. But not everyone has the capacity to connect with their twin flame within this lifetime. Twin flames emerge within our lives when our souls are ready to undergo the process of spiritual awakening and transformation. For some people, the twin flame connection is simply too intense and is not welcome, and hence never happens.

Can a twin flame be a soul mate?

Yes, it is possible that a soul mate can become a twin flame, and vice versa. But twin flames and soul mates have different functions. Twin flame relationships are intense and challenging: their purpose is to help you spiritually grow. Soul mate relationships, on the other hand, are more mild and peaceful: their purpose is to help support you. It's like the difference between fire (twin flames) and water (soul mates).

Why do twin flames run?

Sometimes, our twin flames run away because the connection is too overwhelming and intense for the ego. When the ego is not ready to spiritually evolve, it resists, fights, and tries to escape – this is why twin flames run and try to avoid the relationship. They chase what is more comfortable to them. Meaning, they try to force others to become a twin flame when in all reality, they're not.

Do you only have one twin flame?

Yes, as the name "twin" implies, there is only one other person on this planet who can be called a twin flame. **All types of relationships** provide the opportunity for growth, but twin flame relationships are rare in their ability to help us spiritually evolve and awaken.

Is there such a thing as a false twin flame?

Yes, there is such a thing as a false twin flame. Whether due to our own false perception (it's true that love blinds us) or due to the pretense worn by the other person, it's possible to mistake someone as our twin flame. The best way to know whether someone is a false twin flame is to pay attention to (a) whether they genuinely share the same values as you, (b) if you can be your true self around them, and (c) if there is mutual spiritual transformation.

Are twin flames toxic?

Our twin flames can have toxic mindsets and wounds, but they are not toxic to be around. On the contrary, our twin flames are loving, inspiring, and supportive people to be around. They help us to become the best version of ourselves possible. A true twin flame will have some negative traits, but that will be outweighed by their positive qualities. False twin flames, on the other hand, are toxic to be around and make us feel rotten inside. You will always feel miserable and alone even when you are with them.

Can twin flames fall out of love?

Yes, unfortunately, it is possible for twin flames to fall out of love. However, this is not to say that the deep soul connection will disappear, or the possibility for rekindling love will vanish. It is possible for twin flames to fall in love, fall out of love, and fall in love again. The nature of life is unpredictable, and there is no divine edict saying that twin flames must love each other forever. The purpose of the twin flame relationship is to help us spiritually evolve, and when that goal has been completed, the connection can sometimes disintegrate. However, it is always possible for our twin flames to re-emerge later in life. These twin flames will always be connected in some way.

-SoulMate-

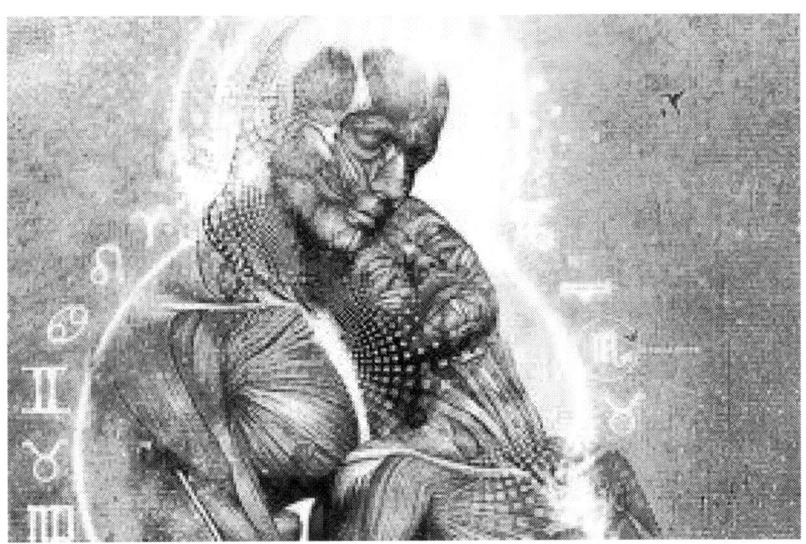

Personally, Eye don't believe that we actually know who our soulmates are because this kind of connection remains attached in the spiritual realm. Just like the scriptures say in most religions, that whatever you bind on earth will be bound in heaven & whatever you loose on earth will be lost in heaven.

For those who actually believe that they can meet someone and know for sure that this person is their soulmate, they will feel it in their soul, even before getting to know them. It's a feeling that you really can't describe, because it's spiritual. Sometimes what the heart and soul feel, the eyes won't see. This can be very risky and tricky because the heart can be deceiving at times.

When you meet that person, one of your soulmates. Let the connection & relationship, be what it is. It may be five minutes, five hours, five days, five months, five years, a lifetime or five lifetimes. Just let it manifest itself the way it is meant to be. It has an organic destiny and this way if it stays or if it leaves, you will be softer from having been loved this authentically. Souls come in, return, and sweep through your life for a myriad of reason. Let them be who and what they are meant to be.

You may ask, "How Do I know if this person can possibly be my soulmate?

You will feel a sense of calm when around them.You spend so much time with your significant other, so being with them should make you feel at home and at peace. Of course, there will probably be butterflies and nerves at first, but after you get comfortable with each other, it should just feel natural. Some of the feelings will be similiar to a person being your twin flame but the soulmate energy is much stronger in the spiritual sense.

You will also have extreme empathy for them.

When they get hurt by someone, you might as well have been hurt too, because, in a sense, you feel each other's feelings. Seeing them upset upsets you, but conversely, you share in each other's happiness. No one is more proud of their bae than you, and when they succeed, nothing makes you happier.

You respect each other. A relationship is nothing without respect, so if your soulmate doesn't admire you for who you are, they're probably not your soulmate. Your soulmate should regard your feelings and ideas, not write them off. They should appreciate and love you and always treat you well.

You share the same life goals. Speaking of the important things...when it comes to life goals, you guys have similar plans. I'm not saying you both want the same career or you want to go to the same college. I'm saying you both agree on where you want to end up after school or whether or not you want to start a family. Obviously, there will be disagreements, but you guys agree on the big stuff. That's a pretty good predictor for longterm happiness with one another.

Being in a relationship with your soulmate will cause you to fight for it at all time because there is no end to it. The two can't see themselves without one another so they are never thinking or accepting seperation. They will go as far as getting a therapist or counselor to fix their relationship. But other than that, the two are very secure with one another. They love being around each other just like the bond between two identical twins.

Even physical death cannot keep two soulmates apart if they are meant to be together. If one dies for any reason, then the other will die shortly after. You normally see this within older couples of one dying right after the other.

Soulmates are a symbol of the universal hope that someone will love you unconditionally in spite of your flaws and baggage.

A soulmate is a symbol. It's a symbol of hope, connection and healing (particularly attachment-based healing) that we as humans desire and crave. It's a symbol of feeling that — in spite of our histories, pain, dysfunctional relationship patterns — we will 'click' with someone and will be able to make it work. The soulmate symbol creates hope and speaks to a desire to be loved, seen, heard, understood and to feel worthy. And even more so, a soulmate is the hope that we will be loved, seen, heard, understood and worthy, despite our flaws.

The Art of Love

ASTROLOGY LOVE

Goldyn Akachi

Before Eye begin on the 12 types of the zodiacs lovers, Eye will give you a brief summary and insight on astrology.

The stars impel; they don't compel. What does compel is the force of your will, and astrology is a tool for helping you get in control of it. Palmist will tell you that the lines on your hand can change in a matter of days. Tarot readers will tell you that you can alter the meaning of your cards. And any good astrologer will tell you that there really are no negative transits.

Despite what you may feel, plametary energies are totally impersonal. The way you deal with these energies as they radiate in your life is nothing but a matter of your choice. It is your choice whether you will allow these energies to work for you. Never think that the power of the planets is stronger than the power that already exist within your own mind. Astrology is important, not because it tells you what is about to happen, but rather because it illuminates what is already there.

Remember, before the planets can guide you to a happier and more fulfilled existence, you must first allow it to happen.

There are four elements in the Universe: Fire, Air,

Earth & Water. These elements in combination make up our total experience. When someone says that he is a fire sign or a water sign, for example, what he is saying is that the position of the sun at his birth fell into one of these categories. Each of the elements has specific properties that identify an individual with a mode of behavior.

"FIRE"

FIRE IS AGGRESSION, ENERGY, ENTHUSIASM, WARLIKE QUALITIES, FEARLESSNESS, COURAGE, STRENGTH, SELFISHNESS, RESTLESSNESS, INSENSITIVITY, ANIMATION, VITALITY, ACTION, PASSION, LEADERSHIP, TEMPERAMENTAL BEHAVIOR, WILLFULNESS.

"AIR"

AIR IS INTELLECT, LOGIC, COMMUNICATION, CHANGEABILITY, SUPERFICIALITY, SOCIABILITY, ENTHUSIASM, TENTATIVENESS, CAPRICIOUSNESS, EMOTIONAL DETACHED, ADAPTABILITY, ARTICULATION, ANALYSIS.

"EARTH"

EARTH IS PRACTICALITY, PERSERVERANCE, BUILDING, MATERIALISM, STRUCTURE, REALIZATION, CONSERVATION, CAUTION, MATERIAL CREATION, STABILITY, STRENGTH, DURABILITY.

"WATER"

WATER IS EMOTION, LOVE, INTUITION, FEELING, PSYCHIC ABILITY, EMPATHY, MOODINESSS, INTROVERSION, MEDIUMSHIP, OCCULTISM, WARMTH, CREATIVITY, ARTISTIC ABILITY, SENSATIVITY, COMPASSION, SELF-SACRIFICE, WISDOM, HEALING ABILITY, JEALOUSY, MANIPULATION.

-THE (ARIES) LOVER-

March 21-April 19 (FIRE SIGN)

You are romantic, dramatic, and daring. You adore the drama of the first glance, the smoldering flirtation, and the larger-than-life love.

You want to be swept off your feet by a bold, delicious, seductive soul who craves as much constant action as you do.

You need someone who will build up and fortify your ego, tell you're extremely grand, and love you for your accomplishments. (You still haven't learned to love yourself for simply what you are. That's why you boast so much.)

You want to hear bells ring, see canonns go off, and be blinded by all the excitement. However, when you wake up, and the champagne looks like stale beer, then you quickly consider cutting out and seeking some action elsewhere.

You are far more attracted to the superficial aspects of falling in love than you are to the commitment for better or for worst. You want a love life that is never stagnant, with a constant array of new faces that appear on the scene to prevent you from admitting that you're bored.

You don't believe that there is merely one love that proves itself to be perfection. Instead, you like to live for the moment and leave yourself open for anyone exciting who comes tearing along to get your attention.

Basically, you feel that variety is more than the spice of life; it's the electrifying principle of existence. Therefore, the more, the better, and you hope that they just keep coming, since you have the courage to handle very many.

You are a highly sexual animal who strives for the satisfaction of it's needs, and its need are really rapacious. You appreciate a lover who is as sexual unhibited and as direct as you are. However, should you encounter someone to whom you are attracted, who doesn't exactly mainline a path to your feet, you have not the slightest hesitation in taking the initiative. This might mean grabbing an elbow, staring relentlessly, knocking someone down in the midst of your enthusiasm, or just bluntly blurting out what you really want.

You're attracted to the aggressive, flashly sort who boast of so many accomplishments that you'll never have to worry about being associated with a loser. You would most like to be devastated by the drug of romantic excitement. However, lacking this, you'll settle for someone who will inflate your ego without being too obvious with it. In your book, arguing is just a waste of time, and time is of essence. If you have to constantly remind someone that you're still alive, it's better that you just forget the whole thing. You believe in making the most of every moment, and for every romantic moment of your life, you certainly have a lot to remember.

The basic problem here is that you are both loving and freedom-loving, and this does not make for the most stable marriage.

-THE TAURUS LOVER-

April 20- May 20 (Earth Sign)

In love you are earthly romantic. You are emotional, sensual, pragmatic, and never feel totally complete without a partner. At times, you may get yourself into a funk longing for the perfect love and listening to sentimental music while you wait for the phone to ring.

Although you have a hard time showing it, you are highly vunerable, and fear rejection to the point of obsession. If you have a lot of Aries in your chart, you may overcompensate with a cool attitude that keeps you on a safe footing with the world outside.

In any relationship you have to know where you stand; being put in an insecure postion that is neither here nor there, gives you a devastating amount of pain. Unlike the sign Gemini, which considers most interactions intially casual, you hope for the possibility of a relationship very early in the game. In your younger years, dependencies develope that tie you into situations longer than you should be. It's hard for you to abandon the hope that you might be getting something in the future and that all the misery in the meantime is not vain.

You are monogamous to the point of tying up your total being into one person. It's easy to sacrifice your own interests for your partner's or to put your own growth and development in the background while you spend your vital energies hoping, waiting, and wanting.

In general, professional success can never carry the same weight as an intimate relationship with much sharing.

However, if you have been burned just too many times, it is likely that you may seek to sublimate your emotions into career considerations. As you have a strong tendency to seek your value in the outside world rather than in yourself, you may find the approval and recognition from your career that you are lacking in your love life.

Because you are so down-to-earth, you don't insist on being dazzled by a whirlwind romance. Instead, you prefer quiet evenings with homemade cooking and a flicker of candlelight.

You, more than any other sign, know how to transform your home into a love den. It's all calculated to make your lover not want to leave. However, sometimes your tendency to smother can snuff out a strong initial interest on the part of another. Try to remain tender, loving, and alluring without getting to the point where you're pushing your friend on the floor.

In any love scene, you are pleasure-loving, warm, and cuddly. However, at times you have a way of wrapping your arms around another body that can break ribs. Loosen up, let go of the jealous feelings that you cling to, and in the long run you'll not only be a happier person, you'll also be a lot more loved.

Marriage is a must, whether you are male or female. You want to be tucked in at night. You also have the need to feel complete by having a partner. In the deepest part of you, you are on a security search for a lasting situation.

-THE GEMINI LOVER-

May 21- June 20 (Air Sign)

In love, you are the maddening, madcap, and emotionally ambivalent. You want everything at once, or you think you want nothing at all.

The most you give anyone who has a romantic interest in you is audition priviledges. And if you feel the need to yawn too often during the first couple of acts, you just wave at the person away and shout "Next."

In relationships, you worry more about being entertained than you do about loving. You're more critical than a judge for the Miss Universe contest, because you're seeking that perfect package that carries with it the assurance that things look like what they should be.

However, if after a certain number of lonely years as an earthy inhabitant you realize bitterly that you have not found Mr. or Ms. Right, you may decide that you're willing to settle. At this point, since you're so flexible, you may reduce the qualifications you are seeking to sheer brilliance, a startling wit, and a most compelling charisma.

You are highly arroused by an intellect of prizewinning quality. And if someone inquired as to be the personal qualities that made you fall blindly in love, your almost programmed response would be: "The mind." While a great body also helps, you are far more titillated by a pithy retort than by a little love pat in an erogenous zone.

One category, however in which you are the least demanding is that you are soaring to the heights of all the mental pleasure your cerebrum can take, about the last thing you'll damage a relationship looking for its warmth.

For the Gemini mind, love is a dangerous thing. When you receive what you have analyzed as too much, you behave like an aging, fussy, and very obese gourmet whose chatteaubriand for two is served more well done than suits his taste. At that point there is nothing to be done except to send it back to the kitchen, where it really belongs.

When it comes to recieving someone's emotions, you need just the right amount, like the perfect pinch of salt. A little too much attention in your direction, and you feel more burdened than flattered.

It takes your mind a lifetime to understand what you think about feelings. Some Geminis die first, and some just live on, never even realizing that they have any left. However, for this particular kind of Gemini, the lack of emotional awareness is so acute that loving is never even a matter of too late.

Since you are freedom-loving, critical, and something of a flirt, marriage is not exactly a rabid desire. Of all the activities that life has to offer, there are many other things that you would prefer to do rather than to commit yourself to a state of connubial bliss.

Basically, you like a lot of variety in your love life, and are not that inclined to settle down of your own accord. While this, by far, is more frequently seen in the Gemini male, it is also a trait of the Gemini female, but somewhat less so.

-THE CANCER LOVER-

June 21/ July 22 (Water Sign)

Love means everything, and without it you're a miserable person trying to make the best out of things. Most likely, your greatest fear is growing old with no one to love you.

Love is a kind of nourishment that revitalizes your soul and gives you the energy to interact with the world with a greater zest and vitality. You seek to insulate your deepest emotions in a tight bond of trust and sharing.

You are a highly emotional individual who often allows sentiment to saturate your romantic experiences. Therefore, it is not unlikely that you have suffered some bitter disapointments because of your relentless subjectivity.

As a defense against a tremendous vulnerability, you sometimes appear cool, and noncaring. Less intuitive individuals are perplexed by your enigmatic behavior and react defensively to it.

However, the fact is that you're not cold at all. You're merely being cautious, perhaps because you've been hurt too many times.

A difficult love life makes you moody, lackluster, and depressed. The intimate give-and-take of love is your deepest desire, and even when you try to sublimate your feelings rather than satisfy them, you often find life much harder to handle. You have tremendous security needs that seek an outlet in an intense love relationship. And until you find your partner, a subliminal kind of pain seems to fit through you.

The devotion of a vital partner probably means more to you than material things. However, to fulfill your desire you'll need to develope more positive attitudes and an objective outlook.

You have a way of looking at all your lovers as prospective marriage partners and mentally assuring yourself that it's just a matter of time. Meanwhile, the object of your intense affections could be telling you in little ways that the only possibility is a freer kind of love that does not and never will include marriage. However, chances are that you'll make yourself believe that this person is suffering from brain fever and will soon recover his or her sense.

The more your overworked mind moves you away from reality to temporarily satisfy your emotions, the more you suffer in the long run. A prerequisite for a sucessful love relationship is that you have to listen to what is going on around you. And if you don't like what you're hearing, tear your attention away to another person who may untimately satisfy you more. Remember that the end of a relationship is not the end of the world. Rather, it may be the beginning of something better. Stop clinging to the past, open your mind and your heart, and let the future come to you.

Marriage means a lot, since you crave the kind of emotional security that lasts forever. One-night stands are not your idea of emotional satisfaction, even if you had a lot of lovers lining up for your attentions. You heartily believe in "happily ever after" and would like to make it work for you. However, sometimes you try too hard and have difficulty admitting that a bad relationship is destined for failure. When it finally breaks apart, despite your tears, you often become bitter and disillusioned, fearful that you'll never find love again.

-THE LEO LOVER-

July 23- Aug.22 (Fire Sign)

At its best, it's sheer romance; the impassioned glances, the breathless interchanges; the feeling of first love; the feeling of last love; the daily, dramatic fantasies. You love love; but even more, you love romance.

Even for the most supercharged Leos moving in overdrive, life isn't worth living without loving. This is not merely a matter of lonliness, but something more complex. While Virgos claim that you are what you eat, you believe that you are what you attract. And if it happens that you're not attracting.....You are a most idealistic sign, and often create a dream world to shield you from what you don't want to see. Eventually, disillusionment dawns, and the sun suddenly retreats. What is left is a cold, grim kind of person shuffling through a myriad of new projects in an effort to scatter the pain. The most unfortunate fact is that it usually works. In these matters, you are the cowardly lion, and your lack of courage in confronting all the factors in a love situation keeps you from learning, changing, and growing.

In matters of love, the Leo male is most vunerable. He has the largest ego problems in the zodiac, and to get what he wants, he's got to put it all on the line. It becomes a make-it-or-break-it situation, and the only way he knows how to survive the savage insecurity is to boast abominably, to overcompensate by a conspicious non-caring attitude. Take away his toys and tools of wordly career attainment, and what you have is the most vunerable of human beings, cowering under two stiff lips and a lot of self-righteous attitudes. He needs love desperately, but he'll never say it. It's infinitely more masculine to scream, shout orders, and throw around the power that society has lent him. "Big" men don't cry, they certainly don't talk about pain, and if they're fast and fortunate enough, they're much too busy even to remember they have feelings. Is it a wonder that so many Leo men really "make it"?

The Leo female is far more flexible, because her ego needs are easily gratified and her emotions are ambivalent. This is certainly the most flirtatious sign. But while Mr. Leo can heartily indulge in the sport only if there's someone securely waiting in the background, Ms. Leo can live from one flirtation to the next without the personal props. Certainly, she would like love, but unlike the Leo male, a life attachment is far from her first priority.

It's the power that makes her pulse race and often leads her down the wrong path. This girl thinks in superlatives, and because she's so sly, self-possessed, and sexually magnetic, she gets what she wants, but only on the surface. Somehow, there's always something missing: she has the chinchilla, but no communication; the president of General Motors just proposed, but he's unbearably boring; she's involved in a mutual intoxication with an international intellect, but he has no emotions. In spite of herself, she finds the kind of consuming love that will last a lifetime, but his income won't last a month. So it's back to the half-hearted flirtations with famous faces.

With the most dazzling lovers, the Leo lady is lonely.....so she keeps it moving, is often promiscuous, and has a deap-seated fear of settling down. Like the Leo man, she sublimates her emotional disatifactions by driving herself toward public prominence. Until this is attained, she is strong enough to survive on superficial encounters. The key to her strength is in knowing that she is her own mother and that all love proceeds from what she gives. Her weakness comes when she can't cut the cord and see that she is too self-dependent.

In general, Leo is a loving sign, with generous, warm, and paternalistic qualities. When both sexes work to transcend their self imposed limitations, there is a great potential for many joyful love experiences. There is also an expansion of the creative drives that tend to dry up during each emotional malaise. When a Leo is in love, everything is easy. But when a Leo seeks to deceive the emotional self, the price is that life somehow becomes even more hard.

Your need for love, approval, and affection will push you in the direction of marriage. However, whatever happens after the moment of the vows can be quite another matter. Your ultimate benefit from marriage depends on where you want it to take you.

-THE VIRGO LOVER-

Aug.23- Sept. 22 (Earth Sign)

When it comes to your love life, you're a critical and fussy perfectionist who could probably even find something wrong with something perfect. However, should someone's mind be profound enough to attract your total attention, then you're willing to overlook some minor flaws.

Basically, you want love more than anything else you can think of. However, there are alot other things that you don't want along with it. First impressions are crucial, therefore crude, immature behavior or game playing can close your mind to granting a second chance.

Although you can appear cold, aloof, and unduly

critical, you are, in fact, shy and supersensative. "Nothing ventured, nothing gained" would never be your motto, since you are so protective of your self-image that you would rather withdraw altogether than stand the chance of surrendering your self-respect.

A fine mind is the first thing that attract you, and after that, warmth and human consideration rate very high on the list. What you desire most is to feel cherished and needed. In return, you are willing to devote yourself to the welfare of the one you love.

Your love life has a very important place in your daily existence, and when it is lacking, you tend to compensate through overwork. However, there is no denying that although intellectual accomplishments can pick up your spirits like a dry martini, there is nothing like coming home to someone you love to give your life a vibrant luster. You seek expansion through love, and ironically, you find it when you least expect it, since it's one area of your life you can't plan, order, or organize.

Marriage is a symbol of the emotional security that you seek and is definitely an expectation. In general, you're a person of serious intentions who finds superficial encounters unsatisfying.

-THE LIBRA LOVER-

Sept.23- Oct.22 (Air Sign)

Falling in love with love is one of your favorite pastimes. The history of the Libra personality is *"L'amour amour toujours..."*

At the deepest part of you, you seek the beatitudes of romantic bliss. However, it often appears that you are far more in love with the idea of love than with the actuality.

You have a refined, idealistic nature that holds stock in the myth of "happily ever after." And this is not to say that two people can't be. However, it always takes at least a little work and many confrontations to come about. Especially in your early years, you cling to the fantansy of being swept away by an uncontrollable force that just starts to accommodate itself in your life. If, from this point, things start to go wrong, you either lose interest or feel hopeless, depressed, and overcome by the pain.

Basically, you want to hear bells ring. You also wouldn't mind a few lights going on at the same time. Anyone who can create this situation for you can occupy a secure place in your life for as long as the bells and lights last. You are attracted to a strong, forceful personality the reeks of both stability and charisma. However, when Cupid calls, you come running, and sometimes the situation is far from ideal.

The deepest part of you seeks to complete yourself in a union with another person, and until you find that missing link, you never feel totally fulfilled. Because your emotional needs are tremendous, you have a hard time making it through life alone.When one partnership ends, it's a relativity short time before you find another one, and sometimes you treat your lovers like replaceable parts.

You tend to have strong feelings of dependence that you project onto the person whom you become involved, and then you start to see life as a matter of "we" instead of "Eye"(I). However, until you are ready to exist in a relationship more as a complete person than as a clinging vine, your satisfaction will always be constricted by your anxiety.

When you put all of your energies into one person, you stand to lose a lot if it doesn'twork. Therefore, you tend to get stuck in painful spaces that only you have created.

Try to remember that the more you expand your inner resources, rather than waiting for it all to come to you, the more you develope yourself, the less you have to lose in any relationship. Until you learn the lesson of selfreliance, the experience of love will be more of a compulsion than a creative emotional situation. Open your awareness to the limitness universe you live in, and try to transcend your frail ego to get to a place of peace you need never relinquish.

At some point or another, marriage is a must, since you nurture a profound need for shared experience. However, because you also seek an abstract ideal, in the long run you may emerge disillusioned.

It is not uncommon for Libras to have more than one marriage, because the feelings in the first one mysteriously deteriorate. However, whether or not any marriage will be lasting really depends on your realistic assessment of your own values.

-THE SCORPIO LOVER-

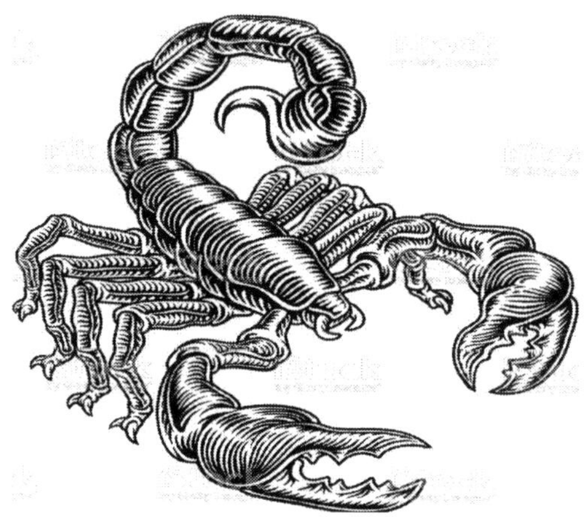

Oct.23- Nov.21 (Water Sign)

If you are a female scorpio, you may be both more mysterious and more vulnerable than your male counterpart. While he can sublimate his emotions through career, sexual manipulations, and athletic undertakings, you're generally not satisfied with less than intense, more meanigful kind of love.

You are loyal, giving, and can appear to be placid even when your emotions seem to be ripping your mind into bite size pieces. At the same time, you are reluctant to lose control until you have shrewdly assessed the odds in every romantic situation. Unfortunately, sometimes your desires get the best of you, and you may find yourself emotionally tied to a brutal affair with no clear recollection of how you really got there.

Your sex appeal is quiet, yet exciting, and seduces from your eyes. Your direct gaze and smile are imbued with a sensuality they can move a man to lust in less than a minute. Yet unlike your Scorpio brother, promiscuity is not your emotional forte. You seek security, tenderness, and trust, and for what you desire, you're willing to give all of yourself in return.

You are both more sensual and more sexually inventive than the Scorpio male, who may be more interested in the ultimate orgasm than in the total experience of lovemaking. However due to your need for control, it may take you years to experience your sexual potential. Because your intense enter into every act, a subconscious fear of abandonment may block both your emotional and sexual reponses for quite some time.

Once in love, you tend to be both possessive and jealous and drown in unresolved emotions long after an affair is over. You often tread a very thin line between love and hate, passion, and violence, even if the feelings are merely confined to your private fantasies.

At a very early age you realize that sex is power and that it will get you whatever you want to go. The

Scorpio experience of loving will take you in many emotional directions in one lifetime. Just remember at each crossroads, you made that decision to be there.

The Scorpio male is a warrior, especially in love, but unlike Martian sibling, Aries, usually battles against his partner rather than for her. If you are a male Scorpio, you probably operate all your romantic endeavors from a mental control panel whose emotional switch is often on "off." You are so inscrutable and emotionally maddening that a bad involvement with you is enough to send a sweet thing to a mental institution. Although you have a lot of loyalty, in affairs of the heart you are really no prize. You seldom compliment, rarely communicate, and keep your feelings carefully closeted until the object of your affections is ready to sign her life away. You want it in all writing, her signature in blood, and someone so farsighted she can't even read between the lines. Should she ever betray you, despite the legitimacy of the contract, she's in for the kind of murder that's so quick and silent that it's really quite painless. The worst possible penalty is you let her live, because what she faces then is the horendous three C's; emotional cutoff, calculated revenge, and the cold glance of death. Your eyes can create such a frigid ambience that she will nervously contemplate changing to her granny underwear.

Although you expect a kind of active devotion that exceeds the ground rules of the Mafia, you often employ double standard in regard to your own behavior. Emotionally, you are still being loyal to your loved one when you are in bed with someone else only for sex. Of all the signs, only you can seperate your emotions from your sexuality and come out the winner. However, God help the loser, especially if she finds herself suddenly emotionally involved.

Not only can you tread over someone else's emotions, you have a unique way of dragging your feet as you go. Although you are an intensely emotional human being yourself, you have an uncanny ability not to let that get in the way when you want something. You can be the most remorseless exploiter of a sexual situation and the most glacial participant in a moment of afterglow. When you've gotten what you want from someone you sexually desire rather than feel for, the first order of business is that the body be removed. You have only one objective: getting your own or your lover's body out the door....quietly.

Unless you are deeply involved and emotionally committed, any woman who tangles casually with you just may get her heart torn out. You are the most maddening kind of egnima, especially to the Taurus woman, who watches her telephone rather than her television, agonizing about whether she's ever going to hear your voice again.

Being sly, silent type, you never volunteer any kind of commitment until the other person has sweated it out far more than just a little, but you are most likely to get caught up by the challenge of someone who is as sly, shrewd, and sexually cunning as yourself.

What you like is being stimulated on several levels, the more the better. You heartily enjoy an insightful intellect who sees through your emotional tactics. You adore a woman who can look you straight in the eye, smile, with a long visual contact. But what really carries you away is someone with all of the above who seems to have a power over you: a special knowledge, or an experience in a Scorpio subject, such as medicine, psycology, or some phase of the occult. Ideally, you would like to learn from a profound love experience and fantasize about a situation that is limitless in its levels of excitement.

Although you need love, falling in love is not an easy experience. Your need for total control as well as your critical nature can often lead you to impose limitations on many love experiences and to kill them slowly before they come to fruition. Although in your silent way you usually wear down and overpower those around you. What you want most is to be overpowered, but through subtlety rather than force.

At this point your extreme jealousy can evoke many sickening moments, much to your specious sense of regret. Since what you crave most is intensity, if you can't find it in pleasure, you'll finally settle for it in pain. Much like Leo, you tend to mentally dramatize the more emotionally intense moments of your life, and once you feel that your sense of pride is succumbing to a debilitating state of affairs, you cut loose with one quick blow. When you wish to end an affair with someone you're losing feelings for, you have a way of becoming invinsible, so that the poor woman might wonder if you were murdered on your way home the last time she saw you. But if your desire is to withdraw in a position of power, you can derive particular glee, even if you're in pain, by informing your former friend that you suddenly decided that it's curtains.

The most lethal trait of the Scorpio nature is the ability to make a former lover feel that she's swimming around an island in shark-infested waters. Emotionally, the Scorpio Man can easily be a foggy island in the middle of a deep dark sea. The undercurrent is so strong, it can draw in unsuspecting souls. The only survivors in these waters are other warriors. Even good swimmers should beware, since life jackets have a way of getting torn apart.

Although you may feel that marriage is a necessity, your partner often feels it to be a situation that must be gotten out of. Why? Perhaps because your spouse has been chained to the bed too long and developed both welts and bedsores.

Your need to use marriage as an emotional base out of which you operate for all of your other activities may cause you to choose a partnership you later regret. Although in all your other dealings you are such a shrewd and far-seeing fox, in the area of marriage, your empotional, sexual, and material needs can easily overcome you.

-THE SAGITTARIUS LOVER-

Nov.22- Dec.21 (Fire Sign)

You are independent, freedom-loving, and forever looking for a challenge. Your romantic reverie is far more an excursion into the exotic than an earthbound evening of champagne and roses. You would rather share a slow boat to China than confine yourself to a candlelit restaurant with a piano player. Because you are so restless impulsive, and looking for the wildest kind of excitement, you're not an easy person to be in love with.

If you are a male Sagittarius, you can be furious when it comes to making a commitment. You are freedom fanatic and a philanderer, and you run rather than walk into lives of a plethora of women. Each one of them you view as a kind of adventure, like going sailing without your life preserver.

In general, your interest is instaneous but has the life span of a flash cube. That is because your attention is too short but your mind is so overstimulated. In a most exuberant way, you yearn to embrace all experience. But because your arms reach out so wide, it all seems inevitably to slip through.

There are some who might accuse you of being adverse to love. However, this really insn't true. The fact is that you tend to be too insensative to even consider being considerate. You live for what you can gain in the moment, rather than for what you can give, and see love as a floor show that comes straight to you.

Because you are always searching and hoping, but haven't found the faintest idea of what you really want, you can go through more women than a greedy sultan. Love is something that you can never seem to understand, because you can't sit still long enough to think about it. Each woman in your life is no more than a rushed experience fitted in between a few others.

Since your love life is busier than the office of a casting director, you have a hard time being monogamous or faithful. Therefore, marriage is not exactly your answer to attaining bliss. You loathe confinement and regard emotional commitment as manacing.

Until you grow up and take the time to acquire a sense of responsibility, you'll remain a roving playboy who always wonders if he could have done a little better. And your view of women will be nothing more than that of a side trip on the way to a circus.

If you are a female Sagittarius, you are less consumed by the chase and more by the quality of an experience. While you are also impulsive, independent, and enamored of adventure, you are capable of making a commitment, should the right man come along.

You prefer an exciting man who respects your independence and sparks your interest with his enthusiasm. It's not at all necessary that he have a private airplane. Merely a strong sense of humor and an assertive nature will do nicely.

You are a passionate person who doesn't find a loving situation a compromise to your sense of freedom. Instead, you find that it's even more fun to have a permanent tennis partner, or hiking companion.

In love, you're not looking for a millionaire who

will place a diamond bracelet around your wrist. You're looking for a funny friend who's a joy to be with. You could care less if he arrives in hiking boots. What do you care about is his sincerity and his soul.

In the end, any man you finally love has to become aware that he's very lucky. You are loyal, loving, and have an invincible life force that could raise the Druids from their resting place. Living with you is like taking a trip far beyond where the normal mind can see.

When it comes to marriage, you may have more than many. You are an adventurer with a freedom-loving philosophy that can take you through many places and many people.

-THE CAPRICORN LOVER-

Dec.22- Jan.19 (Earth Sign)

Although you're a baracuda in the business world, you're shy and vulnerable when it comes to loving. A deepseated sense of insecurity can often make a love situation for more painful than pleasurable.

Despite that you possess a remarkable sense of realism in most areas, in matters of romance it is not unusual that you go through an intiatory period with the wrong people. Because you get sidetracked by stunning surface qualities, you often set yourself up for a bad hurt. And because you're not the most resilent human being, emotional pain can hang on long after an affair is over.

Often you have to endure many difficult love situations before you come to conclusion that "Love is all." A less than total love might be great for a freedom-loving Aquarius or for a Sagittarius with a short attention span. However, the compromise of a partial love for you, despite the satisfactions it may bring in the beginning, will, in the long run, only make you ill-tempered.

Because you have deeper emotional needs than an Aquarius or a Sagittarius, it's important from the onset that you don't sell yourself short. You have a terrible tendacy to be too patient and to settle for unsatisfactory conditions in the present rather than create change by making clear, forceful demands. What holds you back is the fear that your demands may not be met and you may lose all. However, you should learn with age that there can be no loss of that which you didn't want in the first place.

When you fall in love, you are serious and, in turn, need to be taking seriously. You find games loathsome, and immature behavior only turns you cold. As a rule, you tend to be faithful, and demand the same from the one you love. When your trust is violated, bouts of jealousy can make your mind constrict in pain.

A warm, stable, affectionate person is your best

choice for a happy relationship. It would also help if the person works as hard as you do. However, the most important factor is that in any relationship you must never neglect your emotional needs. Remember that for another to respect your needs, you must first show a little respect for yourself. Only you create your romantic limitations, and once you grow beyond the need to do this, you are ready for the kind of love that will flourish.

Although you're definitely the marrying kind, often you don't marry until you're a mature adult. Ideally, you seek a partner who represents a bastion of security and stability.

-THE AQUARIUS LOVER-

Jan.20- Feb.18 (Air Sign)

You're the truly independent sort who creates a comfortable space and stays at a safe distance. Therefore, your attitude toward love is just like you, unconventional.

Your feeling is: "The more I don't see you, the more I want you." You stay away from predatory people who might close in and cut you off from that feeling of freedom that is so precious.

Soft lights and mood music don't move you half as much as somebody intelligent to talk to. The more interests, the better, since you're seeking the mental stimulation that arises from a vital, inquisitive person. Because your attitude toward love is more celebral than emotional, you have to like the idea of a person before you can come to a point of loving. Admiration is a key factor to your emotional makeup and the more someone gives you the reason to feel it, the more responsive you spontaneously become.

Basically, you're looking for someone to share your passion for photography, body painting, and nuclear physics. Or, even better, you'd like someone who also has many passions to share. Falling in love for the Aquarius means having a mind so stimulated that the body is forgotten.

Even in love, you're detached and freedom-loving, which may madden and confuse a possessive lover. You probably see your lover as your best friend and find flowery language and effusive romanticism excessive. Basically, you find so much drama and excitement in the details of daily life that you don't feel the need to impose grade-B-movie standards on your love relationship.

Because you're an idealist, in your own idiosyncratic way you're also romantic. However, most people neither see this nor understand it. When you do love, you embrace all a person's faults and virtues, without illusion and without a cumpulsion for reform. Your attitude is that the greatest gift you can give a human being is respect for individual freedom. When the lovelight shines in your eyes, it seems to say "I accept you as you are, and I know what that is." In return, you require the same mental, emotional, and physical space. But if the moment should come when your lover seems to be encroaching on your own space, with no intention of moving, it is time to say in that characteristic Aquarian way, "Let's be friends." Alas, the door is reopened, the air is cleared, and once again you can feel your energy moving.

Because you're such a freedom-loving person who enjoys crowds as much as one-to-one situations, marriage is certainly not the end-all and be-all of your existence. Many Aquarians marry late in life, and some not at all. However, those who do settle into a connubial state cannot be confined if the marriage is to last.

-THE PISCES LOVER-

Feb.19- Mar. 20 (Water Sign)

Although you often loath your vulnerable side, you're a wild romantic, itching for emotional intensity. You want your soul to be swept away by nothing less than a grand passion.

You're a highly charged sensualist who'd love to live out a fantasy. However, in such situations you often let your emotions get the best of you. You're an emotional attached lover living in the dream of how exquisite your life could be if only....

Needless to say, you're an idealist who is both dreamy-eyed and devoted to the act of loving. However, this problem is that too often you become enslaved by negative situations and hang on to the past like a drowning swimmer embracing a sinking boat. When you really want someone, you'll sit back and wait interminably, feeling that time will be able to change conditions that you can't.

When your romantic life is really wretch, you get dreary and depressed, and feel lonely, unloved, and alienated. The next step is to seek escape through drinking, drugs, sleeping, eating, promiscuous sex, or overwork.

On your more devastating days, you seek solitude. One of your favorite things is to crawl under the covers and curl into a ball, feeling sorry for yourself and wishing the world wouldn't be so unsparing. At this point, the pain is so intense that it almost becomes a kind of pleasure.

However, when the time comes that you feel like a bitter, jaded, loveless victim, remember that it was you who made all the choices. In compromising a sense of total satisfaction in order to gain emotional security that existed only in your mind's eye, somehow you lost. On the other hand, maybe you learned something. In the end, your love life is merely a statement of what you think you deserve. Therefore, if you're not getting what you want, maybe you should just stop crying about it and decide not to settle till you get it.

Because you have a roaming eye and forked tongue, marriage is not always your best bet. Monogamy can be a problem, especially if you choose a mate who might murder you in a moment of sweet revenge.

Wisdom, Gems, Affirmations & the Laws of Love

The Art of Love

YOUR FIRST
EXPERIENCE WITH TRUE-LOVE
IS ACCPETING WHO YOU TRULY ARE

BE WILLINGLY TO CARE
FOR SOMETHING OR SOMEONE OTHER THAN YOURSELF

SACRIFICE, EVEN IF IT MEANS YOUR LIFE

PAY ATTENTION TO MENTAL & SPIRITUAL ENERGY
WHILE ESTABLISHING LOVE CONNECTIONS WITH PEOPLE

LOVE BY ACTION, BY ANY MEANS NECESSARY

COMBINE PLEASURE WITH PAIN

ALLOW THEM TO HATE YOU FOR WHAT YOU ARE &
LOVE YOU FOR WHAT YOU ARE NOT

HATE IS UNORTHODOX LOVE

KEEP THEM EXPECTING AND WANTING MORE, BUT GIVE
LESS.....ENOUGH TO SATISFY

BE THE OPPOSITE OF WHAT THEY ARE USE TO BUT
ALWAYS BE THERE WHEN THEY NEED YOU

BE BOLD, HONEST & NEVER ASHAMED TO LOVE

Goldyn Akachi

A WOMAN CAN HAVE A THOUSAND MEN COMPLIMENT HER ON HER BEAUTY
BUT IF SHE DOESN'T TRULY BELIEVE WHAT THEY ARE SAYING WITHIN HERSELF
THOSE THOUSAND COMPLIMENTS WOULDN'T MEAN ANYTHING & WILL ALWAYS BE OVERPOWERED BY THAT ONE MAN WHO MADE HER FEEL UGLY

A WOMAN COULD HAVE SEX WITH HUNDREDS OF MEN
BUT SHE WILL ONLY REMEMBER THAT ONE MAN THAT SHE MADE LOVE WITH

A WOMAN IS AT HER BEST WITHOUT WORRY
A WOMAN LOVES FOR A MAN TO TAKE CARE OF HER
IT IS THE LOVE OF SECURITY, RELAXATION, & PEACE THAT SHE FALLS IN LOVE WITH, NOT THE MAN HIMSELF
HER LOVE FOR THAT MAN IS BUILT THROUGH TIME & INNERSTANDING
NO MATTER HOW HARD THE WOMAN WORKS OR HOW INDEPENDENT SHE SEEMS TO BE
SHE WILL NEVER BE AT HER FULL PEAK OF LOVE IF HER TIME IS LIMITED TO GIVE & TO RECEIVE THE FRUITS OF LOVE

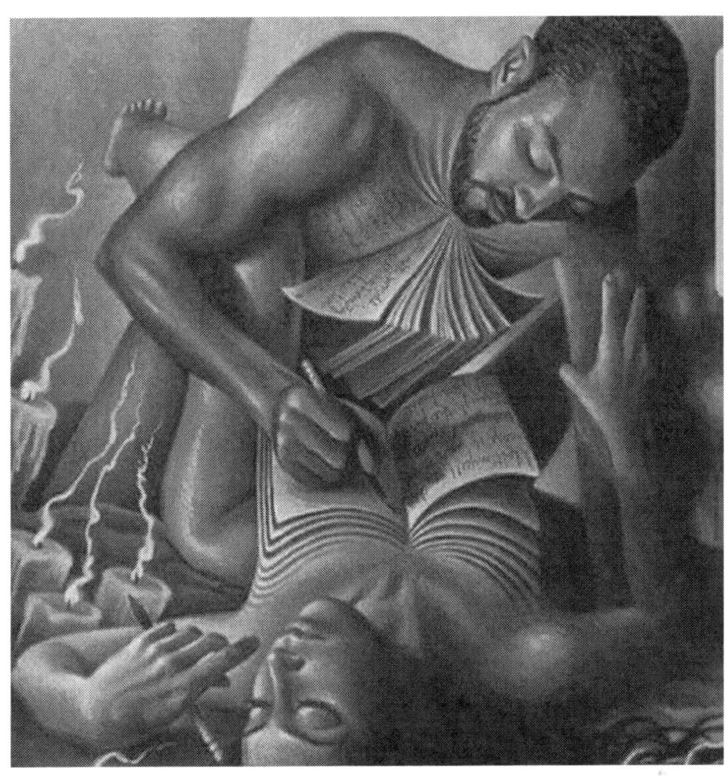

EVERYONE HAS A STORY, SO IN ORDER FOR A PERSON
TO REALLY FEEL, INNERSTAND, & LOVE YOU,
YOU MUST BE WILLING TO OPEN YOUR BOOK(HEART)
UNTO THEM.
NEVER BE ASHAMED OR TOO AFRAID OF WHAT IS
WRITTEN, BECAUSE YOU MAY INTERACT WITH SOMEONE
WITH A SIMILIAR STORY THAT IS ALSO IN SEARCH OF
A BETTER CHAPTER.
OUR HEART'S STORIES ARE EVERLASTING,
IT EXISTS OF ALL TRIALS & TRIBULATIONS FILLED

WITH HAPPINESS, JOY, & PAIN.
WHATEVER YOU DO, ALWAYS KEEP YOUR HEART(BOOK) OPEN & CONTINUE WRITING.
IN EVERY STORY, WE SEEK THE PERFECT ENDING & IT'S OUR RESPONSIBILTY AS THE AUTHOR TO ESTABLISH THE OUTCOME.
IF SOMEONE IS COMPATIBLE WITH YOU ON A MENTAL & SPIRITUAL LEVEL, IT WOULD BE WISE FOR YOU TO ALLOW THEM TO BECOME AN OPEN READER OF YOUR BOOK(HEART), FOR THAT PERSON WILL ALWAYS HOLD A SPECIAL PLACE WITHIN YOU.

WHEN YOU GROW ACCUSTOM TO PAIN, IRONICALLY
YOU START BELIEVING THAT'S HOW YOU SHOULD BE
LOVED

STOP CONFUSING LUST FOR LOVE

STOP CONFUSING ATTACHMENT FOR COMFORT

STOP CONFUSING REPEATED APOLOGIES
FOR THE HOPE OF CHANGE

STOP CONFUSING RED FLAGS FOR FLAWS
BECAUSE IF IT WAS MEANT TO BE
IT WOULDN'T BE SO TRAUMATIC

SOMETIMES LOVE IS PAIN AND IT CAN BE VERY HARD
BUT LOVE CAN NEVER BECOME TRAUMATIC
TO A POINT WHERE YOU FEEL
LIKE YOUR DYING INSIDE & OUT FROM DISTRESS.

TRUE LOVE IS NOT ABOUT FINDING YOURSELF IN ANOTHER

THERE'S NO SUCH THING AS FALLING IN LOVE
OR THINKING YOU IN LOVE
BECAUSE YOU WANT TO FIND YOURSELF

YOUR IDENTITY IS NOT TO BE SOMEONE'S OTHER HALF
IT'S TO BE YOUR BETTER SELF

DON'T BE SO SWEPT UNTO YOUR PARTNER
THAT YOU BECOME THEM

KEEP YOUR INTERESTS & HOBBIES
& YOU WILL BE MORE INTERESTING TOO
& INTERESTED IN, YOUR PARTNER

***LOVE** IS AN UNCONDITIONAL COMMITMENT TO SELFLESSLY SERVE, TRUTHFULLY COMMUNICATE, FEARLESSLY PROTECT, GRACEFULLY FORGIVE, COMPASSIONATELY HEAL, AND ENDURINGLY REMAIN IN RELATIONSHIP WITH AND FOR THE SAKE OF ANOTHER.*

Your Daily Affirmations: 1. Eye am surrounded by love every day in every way.

2. My heart is always open to love.

3. All Eye see is love.

4. In life Eye always get what Eye give and Eye always give out love.

5. Eye attract love in abundance.

6. Everywhere Eye go, Eye find love. Life is joyous.

7. Eye love myself.

8. Eye radiate love.

9. Love flows through me.

10. Love shines from within me.

11. MY BUSINESS ALLOWS ME TO HAVE A LIFE EYE LOVE.

12. EYE AM GRATEFUL FOR THE LOVE THAT IS AROUND ME.

13. EYE AM ATTRACTED TO LOVE.

14. EYE AM WORTHY OF GREAT LOVE.

15. EYE SPREAD LOVE WITH MY WORDS, DEEDS, AND LIFE.

16. MY VIBRATION IS LOVE.

17. LOVE WANTS ME.

18. EYE AM COCOONED IN THE LOVING ENERGY OF THE UNIVERSE.

19. EYE AM IN TUNED TO THE FREQUENCY OF LOVE AND ABUNDANCE.

20. EYE AM LOVE!

{THE LAWS OF LOVE}

–You shall love with all your heart, with all your soul, with all your mind, and with all your strength.–

Your Love Shall *Require Commitment*: "The strength of your commitment will always determine the strength of your relationship."

Your Love Shall *Selflessly Make Sacrifices*: "The ultimate test of love comes when a person is asked to give up all they value for the sake of another."

Your Love Shall *Speak Truth*: "Honesty always paves the way to intimacy."

Your Love Shall *Conquer Fear*: "There isn't enough room in your heart for both fear and faith, so each day you must decide which one gets to stay."

Your Love Shall *Offer Grace*: "If we deserved forgiveness it wouldn't be called grace. If we could earn it, it wouldn't be real love."

<u>Your Love Shall *Bring Healing*:</u> "Real peace isn't the absence of tragedy but the presence of a savior who is bigger than your tragedy."

<u>Your Love Shall *Live Forever*:</u> "Realizing death isn't the end should change the way we live and the way we love."

<u>Coherence:</u> The first and most primary relationship we have is with the self in divine union with *"All that is."* ***We are beings of vibration.*** *And the frequency of love carries the harmonic wavelengths that represent the very essence and presence of life.*
Love is so natural a state that we have to be taught the opposite: to *not* love. **And when we look outside of ourselves for love, we've already lost it.**

<u>Benevolence:</u> Love is incorruptible, innocent and sacred. It stands open, naked and empty of any desire. Love is the innocent eye, for it carries no judgments and is the ultimate liberator of all fear. When we give with <u>loving kindness</u>, the heart can truly come alive. Make no distinctions in love. Be ever-mindful and heart-awakened to the awareness that love is ever-

PRESENT. DEVELOP TOLERANCE AND DEEP UNDERSTANDING FOR ALL BEINGS AND YOU WILL KNOW THE TRUE ESSENCE OF LOVE.

INTELLIGENCE: LOVE IS THE APERTURE OF ALL DIVINE THOUGHT. IT RISES AS AN OMNIPRESENT FIELD OF ALL THAT IS. AND WHEN THE TWO MEET, THEY COME INTO UNION. THERE WE HAVE AWAKENING, THERE WE HAVE POWER. **THERE WE EXPERIENCE THE CONSCIOUSNESS OF CREATION.** WE ARE THE LIVING BREATHING UNION OF THESE TWO OVERSEEING PRINCIPLES MERGING WITHIN THE HEART. IN ITS INNERMOST CALLING, TRUTH CAN ONLY BE FELT IN THE HEART. WHY? BECAUSE AS SOON AS IT LEAVES THE LIPS, IT DISAPPEARS FROM SPIRITUAL UNDERSTANDING. **LOVE IS TRUTH AND TRUTH IS THE LOVE**

EVER-PRESENCE: LOVE IS THE GRAND DESTROYER OF ALL ILLUSIONS. IT IS OMNIPRESENT, TIMELESS, AND WHOLE IT CANNOT BE DIVIDED. LOVE IS THE GRAND AWAKENER INTO ALL LIGHT. QUANTUM PRESENCE IS THE LIVING KEY TO ALL STATES OF ASCENDED ENLIGHTENED CONSCIOUSNESS. **LOVE IS THE ESSENCE BEHIND ALL OF CREATION AND IS THEREFORE HOLY AND DIVINE.**

<u>Splendor:</u> In order to truly know love, we must allow it to enter our being and invite it to remain as a permanent state of our presence. Love heals all wounds. It does not seek for another or is desirous of any truth. It is simply the ultimate transmission of an invitation to be. Love is the invitation.

<u>Resonance:</u> Love is the ultimate resilience. It invites us to return to our inherent nature, again and again. It gathers up all of the fragmented parts of our being and slowly merges them into the whole. Love is beyond belief for it needs no proof of its value. **If we learned to love wholeheartedly, continuously, playfully – we would know true value and worth.** There is nothing else but love. When love is present, light descends. And light is the omniscient energy of love's pure heart. Love is at the heart of all creation, literally! Feeling love is the prayer and affirmation of the living cord of the divine matrix of being. **Love is the promise!**

<u>Immanence:</u> Love is the ever-bearing gift that keeps on blooming. It is our ultimate treasury

OF WEALTH AND WISDOM. LOVE ANOINTS OUR BEING WITH THE INVITATION OF LIFE, THE PROMISE OF AWARENESS AND THE GIFT OF WISDOM. LOVE'S UNENDING PROMISE IS A GIFT. AND RECEIVING THE GIFT OF LOVE UPLIFTS OUR BEING. AS WE RISE TO MEET THE ASCENDED DIVINITY AT THE HEART OF AWAKENED, ENLIGHTENED BLISS, "ANANDA" THESE WORDS RING OUT TO ALL..."WE ARE ONE WITHIN THE MANY AND THE MANY WITHIN THE ONE."

"Love Is Like The Wind
You Can't See It
But You Can Always Feel
It."

When the power of LOVE overcomes the love of power the world will know peace.

- Jimi Hendrix

"If Eye Know What Love
Is,
It Is Because Of You."

Made in the USA
Columbia, SC
21 November 2022